Praise for *An Angel by My Side*

'Want reassurance you can trust? Then look no further than Jacky Newcomb, a well-known and highly respected name in psychic circles. Jacky's a brilliant storyteller – and down to earth with a great sense of humour ... This book is a riveting follow-up to *An Angel Saved My Life* and a compulsive read for anyone interested in the afterlife.'

Mary Bryce, Editor of *Chat – It's Fate* magazine

'This is a fascinating book filled with amazing true stories that give reassurance, comfort and enlightenment from the fascinating world of angels. Jacky's compassion and sense of humour will have you hooked from the first page.'

Debbie Dawson, Editor of *The Psychic Voice*

Praise for *An Angel Treasury*

'Jacky Newcomb has compiled probably the most fascinating book on angels.'

Colin Fry, star of LIVINGtv's *6ixth Sense with Colin Fry*

Also by Jacky Newcomb:

An Angel Treasury

A Little Angel Love

An Angel Saved My Life

An Angel by my side

Amazing True Stories
of the Afterlife

Jacky Newcomb
'THE ANGEL LADY'

HARPER element

HarperElement
An Imprint of HarperCollins*Publishers*
77–85 Fulham Palace Road,
Hammersmith, London W6 8JB

The website address is: www.thorsonselement.com

and *HarperElement* are trademarks of
HarperCollins*Publishers* Ltd

First published by HarperElement 2006

10

A catalogue record of this book is
available from the British Library

ISBN-13 978-0-00-724231-3
ISBN-10 0-00-724231-X

Printed and bound in Great Britain by
Clays Ltd, St Ives plc

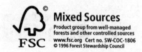

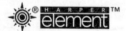

Contents

Acknowledgements

I want to say a big thank you to everyone who has written to me over the years and shared their amazing stories of angel visitations, afterlife communication and many more. Your stories help me to learn and grow on my own journey and of course I love to share them all with you, my readers.

Thanks to Mum and Dad, John, Charlotte and Georgina. Also, to Tigger, my faithful cat and to Lady, may she rest in peace. To my new black kitten Magik – another companion as I write.

Special thanks to Katy and Laura at HarperElement who work so hard on my behalf. Thank you to Fiona, my long-suffering editor, and to Jane and Nicola for your help with my constant pile of readers' letters!

Introduction

I have been on the verge of being an angel all my life
but it's never happened yet.

Mark Twain

'... Thanks Jacky, you are an angel,' people say.

No, seriously I am not. I would like to mention here that I drink copious amounts of beer at my local pub, smoke like a trooper and dance wildly at our local night clubs but that would be a lie, even in the interests of good writing ... actually I am more partial to champagne; usually only visit the local pub for lunch, and don't actually smoke! As for the wild dancing, my teenage children would kill me for sure, so that does take the glamour off my life a little.

Usually at this point I would suggest that I am a 'normal' wife and mother to two teenage girls, but the word 'normal' has now been blasted off the radar. If you've read my other books you will realize that I was plagued by a series of unexplained paranormal experiences from a very young age, and then later explored this phenomenon to actually encourage more. Yes, I enjoyed being psychic.

I realize it's time to be 'more honest' about these paranormal experiences; after all, my massive postbag has shown me that I am not alone. I have a strange life … but then so do many of us. If people think we're weird then so be it. Everything I have written about my life and continue to share is true. I have occasionally changed the names of those close to me for personal reasons but that's about it. I no longer worry about what people might think of me. This is who I am, like me or loathe me – but I hope you like me.

In my earlier books, I shared some of the experiences I had as a child. I used to wake up in my bedroom to see strange 'people-like shapes' floating around, and seriously, it just went downhill from then on … no, I'm kidding! I don't want to bore you if you've already read my story, but for those of you who have not, I'll do a quick re-cap. As a young girl I found myself in difficulties in the sea when I was staying on the Isle of Wight, off the English south coast. I thought I was going to drown when I felt and heard a 'being' who assisted me back to shore, effectively saving my life. Who was this unseen stranger? Was it my angel?

Later, as an adult, I had several 'angel-type experiences'; during one in particular, I actually heard 'angel choir' music. I'd had out of body experiences and bizarre premonitions. These all sent me on a great adventure where I investigated the angel phenomenon, searched and explored out of body experiences and learnt to control some of the things that were happening to me. Knowledge was the key to coping with all things paranormal, so of course I used that as an excuse to buy a lot of books! It was no more difficult to switch off the psychic as it was to switch it on. But of course, you just have to learn how. Some of this phenomenon included meeting and working with my spirit guides and communicating with my loved ones on the 'other side'.

After some of my psychic adventures, I wrote my first two angel books, *A Little Angel Love*, and *An Angel Treasury*. In my third book, *An Angel Saved My Life*, I wrote more about my own psychic adventures and was stunned at the response from people. I had about forty emails with the same phrase, 'I couldn't put it down.' You never believe that your own story is that interesting but apparently it was.

The last few years have been a rollercoaster ride. Writing a book or two changes things in a way. All of a sudden people wanted my autograph. Wow, me? Are you sure? How humbling can that be, but at the same time, what an honour. Knowing that you can touch and affect others on their own path because they've read something you've written is not something you actually think about when you put pen to paper – or in my case, type words into the computer. I've done fifty or so radio interviews, appeared on several television programmes and met and worked with some big names in the paranormal world. I am very lucky to do what I do, and I love it. I thank the angels every day.

It had always been my intention to share the paranormal and angelic experiences of both myself and others in an easy-to-read and down-to-earth way. So many of these experiences were very positive and uplifting, literally at times saving peoples lives. I'm not what you call an 'intellectual type' (did I really write that down…I might wish I hadn't!), so, the easy-to-read theory also means easy-to-write. I have decided to 'tell it like it is' and hope for the best.

One time, I was having a rough day and drove to the local garden centre. I sat in my car for a while because I realized I'd forgotten to bring my purse, and a credit card was not really going to be useful for the single cup of coffee that I had wanted. I sighed under my breath: could the angels help me with this?

A lady in a car parked opposite was frantically waving at me and I smiled. I peered through the windscreen, and wanted to look behind me to see if she was waving at someone else. Did I know her? She came over and knocked on the window and I felt embarrassed. My eyes had been watering all day and I looked as if I had been crying – I wondered if she might think so?

'Hello, are you okay?' she smiled sweetly.

Self-conscious now, I smiled, my cheeks flushing slightly as I explained why I was still sat in the car.

'I'm just going inside for a cup of coffee, could I buy you one?' She asked politely.

Were the angels at work here? Should I know this woman? I only wished for a coffee just a moment ago and it had manifested already. Gratefully, I got out of the car and we talked on the way into the garden centre restaurant. She seemed to know me and apparently I had signed a copy of my book for her. I searched my mind frantically, not wanting to embarrass her.

We strolled over to a table and she explained, talking a little too fast and breathlessly.

'You must think I am a little weird. I wondered if you might even know who I was but I read your column and have all of your books so I feel as if I know you so well.'

Recognition dawned on me as she explained her story. I did remember her – slightly, that is. She'd attended one of my workshops, but it had been over a year ago and we had talked for just one minute. She looked so much better than when I'd seen her last and she explained how she'd had a lifesaving operation since we'd met. We'd spoken as I signed her book and she'd remembered me.

I had needed someone to chat to that day. This lady was the only person I 'knew' in the vicinity and the angels made sure that she was there to listen to me talk and buy me a cup of coffee! I like to think we helped each other as both of us had a lot to say that day. If you're reading this, thank you again.

Can a mum from middle England change the world? Probably not, but she might be able to help with one little corner of it. But then maybe that is the whole point. It's easy to say that one person can't make a difference in the world, but of course they do … and sometimes it's almost accidental. Are you a great gardener? Then make beautiful gardens. Do you love building things? Then build away. Anything which you love and you put energy into will change the world one little bit at a time. I wanted to work on my own little bit as we all do.

Let's go back a bit and I'll bring you up to date. I've spent years exploring the afterlife and all things magical but as with all stories there are moments when life moves forward with a gigantic leap. In this book, I want to share some more of my experiences with you.

Then we will take another look at some of life's angels: angels of the 'winged variety'; our spiritual guides; and our 'angel loved ones' helping from the 'other side' of life. Sometimes our angels are our human or animal friends … are they guided by those of a higher dimension? One of the more fascinating aspects of this book is the stories of afterlife communication; our loved ones in the afterlife popping back to let us know that they are well, happily continuing their lives in the heavenly realms. Some of these stories might seem hard to believe but, as with everything I share with you, it's all true, I promise.

So let's start with chapter one…

Please Note

Several chapters of this book include Jacky's personal story and investigation of the afterlife. This book in no way suggests that readers follow the journey and experiment with afterlife communication in the way that Jacky shares here. Each reader must make up their own mind as to the suitability, relevance and application of afterlife communication and paranormal experience in their own lives.

Still here …
I saw you standing at my grave
… but I'm still here.
I saw you turn and say goodbye, you waved
… but I'm still here.
I heard you call my name as you slept last night,
I felt your pain and fear and fright
… but I'm still here.

I heard you wonder how you'd cope alone
… but I'm still here.
I heard you sob, I heard you moan
… but I'm still here.
I saw you as you held your head in your hands,
With the world still full of your time's demands
… but I'm still here.

I held you in my arms today
… I'm still here.
I felt your response because you knew there was a way
… I'm still here.
I know you felt my hand as it brushed against your cheek,
I haven't left your side, I've been here all week
… I'm still here.

I have a new home where I now reside
… but I'm still here.

Love is still the same from the 'other side'
… and I'm still here.
From time to time I'll pop in and say hello,
I'm really sorry that I had to go
… but I'm still here.

It's my greatest wish that you live each day
… knowing I'm still here.
Life must carry on and I know you'll find a way
… knowing I'm still here.
I promise one day, there'll be an ease to the pain,
And I want you to begin to live your life again
… knowing I'm still here.

You still have so much more of your life to live
… but I'm still here.
Your beautiful soul has such a lot to give
… and I'm still here.
Lots more dancing, singing and fun,
Parties to attend and things to be done
… and remember … I'm still here.

Jacky Newcomb

Part 1

CHAPTER 1

Mystical Mum

How did I get here? What was it about? Was it her smile? Was it the way she crossed her legs, the turn of her ankle, the poignant vulnerability of her slender wrists?

Martin Sage and Sybil Adelman, *Northern Exposure: The Bumpy Road to Love,* 1991

'I've done a lot of research. It's fascinating, and I'm really hooked. Even though people in your family die … they're not dead. I mean they are, but they're not.' I gushed to my dad over coffee one day. He smiled politely.

'I've discovered that spirits have the ability to manipulate energy, especially electrical and clockwork items,' I babbled on. 'It's how they let us know they are still alive!' I added breathlessly.

I think Mum had gone shopping with my sister and Dad always loved a good gossip so I'd driven round the corner to visit him. It really was 'just' around the corner. I was lucky that my parents lived a five-minute walk away but I usually drove as I always seemed too busy to stop and enjoy the short walk, even though I visited them several times a week.

A busy mum with two teenage daughters of my own, I always seemed to be rushing from one project to the next. Books for review were stacked up on my desk and a whole carrier bag full of readers' letters from my magazine column, all with questions about readers' psychic and paranormal experiences, were waiting for personal replies. I was halfway through my third book on angel and afterlife communication experiences, and wary of the looming deadlines, but the research was really exhilarating. I was keen to chat about it to anyone who might listen … or not … and dads always listen, don't they!

I rushed on excitedly about my latest research.

'After our loved ones pass over to heaven, they come back and let you know that they are okay, that they are still alive in some way. I have hundreds of stories now from all over the world, Dad. They come in their spirit bodies and visit people in dreams, and make the lights flicker and things. I really believe that we don't die … at least not in the way that we think!'

Dad looked on kindly. Did he think I was crazy? Bless him, he never said, and he just smiled fondly in the way that dads do.

I'd been sharing a weird story I'd read about a music box. Paranormal, I guess you would call it. A woman had inherited all of her mother's jewellery after she'd died, but couldn't find her mother's precious pearl necklace. Sitting in her mother's home after the funeral, the woman wondered where the necklace might have gone. As she was thinking about the problem, a family music box started playing inside a locked cupboard. It was a musical jewellery box and it had sat in the cupboard, without being wound up, for some time.

The woman opened the cupboard and lifted out the box which was playing inside, and when she opened it up she found the missing pearls inside. The music box had given the clue to where they were hiding. It was a great story but was it just a coincidence? I just loved it.

I looked at my watch and sighed. Wary of the mountain of writing I needed to complete by the end of the day, I picked up my coat and leant over to kiss Dad goodbye, thinking of how much he looked like his deceased brother, Eric. Eric was a cherished and much missed family member.

'When I leave, Uncle Eric will do something to let you know he's been here nosing in on our conversation again today,' I joked. 'You know he will want to show us this is all true.'

As the words left my lips, we heard the smoke alarm give a single bleep and we both burst out laughing. Good timing! Had my late Uncle Eric communicated his visit from the afterlife? I know that he did.

Later on that day, Dad told me he'd checked the smoke alarm just in case, and the battery was fine. Was this a coincidence, or perhaps another piece in the afterlife communication puzzle?

The lights often flickered at my parents' house, and anywhere the family gathered for special events together. If we mentioned Uncle Eric's name the lights would always begin to flash, almost to indicate that he had joined in the family fun. We knew he was with us.

Was it more amazing coincidences or was my uncle really communicating with us from beyond the grave? We were certainly convinced, and each time a light went on and off we all laughed and said, 'Hello Eric.' It wasn't a frightening thing, just a bit of family fun and I guess a great comfort. We never like to think that our loved ones really leave us when they die, and I'm totally convinced they don't.

We felt him around us a lot. I remember another time I was sitting in my living room late one night. It was 1 am and I was snuggled down on the sofa in our dimly lit living room with my head in my hands. I was feeling very distressed about a problem at the small 'new age' store where I worked part time when I suddenly felt the familiar presence in the room with me. I knew it was Uncle Eric. How? I just sort of felt it – you know, in the same way that you 'feel' when someone is looking at you behind your back. Those eyes piercing into your back … you just know.

'Is that you Eric?' I asked out loud. The lights flickered on cue in the living room and I laughed. He had announced his arrival in the usual way.

'Flash the lights once for yes, and twice for no,' I joked. The lights flicked once more. I swear we had a five-minute conversation using the yes/no system before I felt his energy pull away! I can't prove it to you, no one was physically there – but I knew it was him! He'd cheered me up a lot! I knew then it was time for bed. I needed to 'sleep on it', as they say.

The next day I decided that the problem with my shop job was that I needed to not be there. I decided to leave. I needed to concentrate on my writing. Writing was what I wanted to do for a living and I was just getting more and more frustrated spending my day doing something I didn't want to do. The following day I handed in my notice. The shop owner seemed very upset with me but I meant nothing malicious by it, it was a personal decision only. I had to follow my own dreams, I needed to be elsewhere.

The next few days were difficult at work. There was a serious tension in the air but I was sad to leave the staff who had become very good friends. I'd been at the shop for a few months – I actually began working for the owner before the shop even opened. Initially, I'd been looking for a part-time job so that I could still meet people whilst I wrote from home. I didn't want to be isolated totally, and the job in an alternative/new age store seemed the perfect choice.

As the weeks went by I'd ended up doing more and more hours in the shop. I needed to be home to meet the girls after school but due to lack of staff I found myself having to work much later than agreed. As the most experienced member of staff, I became the shop manager by default. I was now beginning to resent the whole thing. I'd only ever wanted to work a couple of days but now my part-time day job was taking over my life and I was beginning to hate it.

Had Eric picked up on my misery when he came and flickered my living room lights that night? I'd wondered whether our relatives on the other side could zoom in on our strong emotions like a distress call; I've since discovered that they do.

I had two more days' notice to work, but when I woke up the following morning, I knew I wouldn't be able to go in that day, but what could I do? I really did feel ill, but felt guilty, too, that I should be working my last two days.

I looked skywards and sighed. 'Angels? Can anyone help me?'

I had no idea who I was talking to in the seemingly empty room but I felt sure that someone, somewhere in the Universe would hear my silent cry!

'If I'm not meant to go into work then I need a big sign and I need it now!'

The phone rang immediately. Seriously – it rang the moment the words left my lips. It was a good friend, a local Reiki healing teacher and she needed my help.

'Jacky, I've had someone let me down for my class. Would you be able to come over? I just need someone to lie on a couch so that my students can practise healing on them. Oh, and I always do a vegetarian home-cooked lunch. You'd be doing me a great favour,' she said. 'I know you've done Reiki I and II before but I thought you might enjoy doing it again.'

I laughed but she'd no idea why. Let me see … go into work or lie on a couch and be 'healed'? I had my answer. Had the angels stepped in, or was it Uncle Eric intervening? I didn't mind either way.

As it turned out, my friend needed my help for both days of her two-day course, so I decided to join in the Reiki class, and then later I did the next course and the next. I was ready for a change of direction. Was this yet another coincidence? Yes, I'd done the healing course before but never had I needed healing more than I needed it at that moment.

We always feel stressed and depressed when we find our lives or aspects of our lives are out of control. Part of my life was out of control. This was definitely one of those times for me. The only way to move forward when we suffer from stress is to change something in our lives; to get back in control of one small aspect of it.

Of course, sometimes we can't control the very thing which is making us depressed. If someone has died, for example, we can't bring them back: all we can do is change the way we feel about it. It's hard, I know.

Mourning the loss of a loved one is a natural thing to do. Some people take years to recover a normal sense of life and others may find that laughter comes again after a few months. It doesn't mean we love them less but we deal with stress in our own way.

Mourning is about feelings of loss for the time we never had together. Moving on is about celebrating the wonderful life they had and the opportunity we were given to share that love for however long or short a time. I wanted to teach the message that I felt my own spiritual helpers were bringing me, but first I had to live some of the lessons myself.

Eric 'called' a lot at that time, and although I never saw him then, it was clear that my little dog Lady could. I felt Eric come into my living room for a visit one sunny afternoon a short while later. It was that same knowing, that same feeling. Something in the very air around me had changed.

'Is that you Eric?' I asked the empty room.

Lady, my Lancashire Heeler, was jumping up and down in excitement and lifted herself up onto her hind legs. She was sniffing and looking at something in mid-air. What could she see? As anyone might, I checked the room for insects or some other distraction but it was clear that the excitement was for something, or someone else!

'If that's you Eric, get Lady to pick up her newspaper chew toy and bring it over here!' I asked, confident of a failure.

Lady was lovely, but not the most intelligent dog in the world. I had given my spirit friend a difficult task indeed … or had I? Lady immediately ran over to her squeaky toy, then jumped back as if someone was there! She rushed at it again and picked it up before turning around and bringing it over to me and planting it proudly on the floor at my feet. Amazing!

I thought about it a lot afterwards. Had my little dog

suddenly learnt a new trick? Had she at that moment understood my words? Had she been wagging her tail at some microscopic fly? No, seriously, whatever way I looked at it, the obvious solution seemed to fit better. She had seen a spirit visitor and followed their instructions rather than my own. Eric was there and although I had sensed my spirit visitor, Lady had actually seen him. I LOVED this!

I've had many encounters with my spirit friends and not just Eric. Eric, because he had been my uncle, was the easiest to recognize when he visited but others also came in 'dreams'.

My first spirit visitation 'dream' was from an old school friend. Guy had died of cancer in his twenties and it was a real tragedy. We grew up together. As soon as he appeared in the dream I immediately became lucid (I was aware that this was not a normal dream and my visitor was actually dead). Even though I was aware that my body was asleep my mind was perfectly awake. This was real, and I knew it was, even at the time.

'Guy! How lovely to see you. Why are you here? You're dead aren't you?'

A short conversation followed about the fact that he had come because he could. I felt like he was testing a new skill. I chatted to my late friend in his spirit body, although I remembered none of the conversation afterwards. I asked him questions about the meaning of life – why are we here and what is our role in life? I obviously wasn't supposed to remember the answers to those. Shame!

I remember asking him, 'Can I pass on a message to anyone for you?' I assumed he had visited me for some higher spiritual reason.

He just told me no, and said it was time to go. Two chairs, me and Guy, sitting in an otherwise empty room – that was it. But even then, I knew it wasn't a normal dream. It was so real, so vivid, so different from a normal dream, and I knew I was talking to a dead person, and that it was okay to be doing so. And that's part of the reason why a 'dream' visitation is used, because we accept things that we would be unable to do in normal waking life!

It was my first dream visitation but it certainly wasn't my last.

CHAPTER 2

I'm Still Here

One cannot help but be in awe when he contemplates the mysteries of eternity, of life, of the marvellous structure of reality. It is enough if one tries merely to comprehend a little of this mystery every day.

Albert Einstein

Eric first introduced himself when he bounced in on a spirit board one afternoon. Well, actually it was a table full of felt-tip letters, A–Z, and the words 'yes' and 'no' stuck around a table at the home of a local medium, but it was the same principle. My sister Debbie and I had gone along for a reading on the recommendation of a friend. I'd had readings before at psychic fairs but I'd never been very impressed. This time would be different, I knew it.

I'd never met the medium, but I'd had the strangest urge to take her some flowers. I 'saw' something specific in my mind's eye, a potted miniature rose. When I got to the shops I went to buy my usual white flowers but was drawn to the yellow roses. Why was I buying flowers for a woman I'd never met?

On the way over in the car, Debbie and I chatted about which of our deceased loved ones we were hoping to visit. Would any of our relatives really come and chat to us through the medium?

Perhaps our Nan would come through or maybe Mum's lovely friend Pat who had passed just six months before, and was still very much in our minds. Wouldn't it be great if Uncle Eric made an appearance? He was such a funny man and we missed him such a lot. We chatted excitedly about what might or might not happen, and in no time at all we pulled up outside the medium's house.

Sandra was a small lady and she explained how she'd been 'poorly'. She made us a cup of tea in her very tiny kitchen, and as an unexpected bonus Sandra had her friend Janice helping out for the night. It looked like we were going to have two readings for the price of one.

Embarrassed, I handed over the plant to Sandra. She seemed pleased but confused. I found myself mumbling about how I'd felt drawn to buy her the flowers but I didn't know why. The medium explained that a dear friend of hers had always bought her yellow flowers when she'd visited. She felt that the roses were a gift from 'spirit'. I wondered if a passing spirit had manipulated me into buying the plant or if it was a wild stretch of my imagination. Perhaps it was just me after all?

Janice waited patiently before handing Debbie and me

a sheet of paper each. Each sheet had a circle drawn in the middle. We were intrigued as pots of paint sat on the table. She sat us down and had us drop splats of paint into the middle of the paper. We had no idea what we were doing or why, but it was a lot of fun. She carefully folded the paper in half and smoothed the two sides together before opening them up and giving us both a reading based on the smears of paint on the paper. I have to say that it just looked like a big smudge of colour to me but she seemed to see something else.

'Look at the angel shape on the paper,' said Janice (I couldn't really see it). 'Look, can you see, it looks like angel wings ... and lots of purple, that's a very spiritual colour.'

Hmm, interesting. She wasn't to know that I had already started collecting angel stories with the idea that one day I might write a book. Maybe she could read something in the paint after all. How disbelieving I was in those days.

We hadn't yet finished our tea but as we'd finished our paintings we were keen to get on with our other reading. We followed the medium and her friend upstairs to a small bedroom with a sofa, a smaller armchair and a collection of small tables; there were even chairs and a cupboard crammed into the tiny space. This was the reading room.

She looked so normal. I guess I didn't know what to expect but if I'm honest I suppose I was a little surprised she wasn't wearing a purple cloak with stars on it and a pointy hat. Sandra started her reading.

'I have a woman here. She's quite snooty, stuck up. No,

that sounds rude and I feel embarrassed now that I know she can hear me say that. Sorry, love. I don't mean stuck up, I mean posh. Oh dear … well, you know what I mean.'

We laughed and she continued.

'She's very well dressed and she's showing me that she liked nice things and expensive holidays.'

We both leaned forward on the tiny sofa. This was good stuff and we looked at each other before nodding in agreement. This person sounded familiar.

'She's showing me a ring.'

'Um, maybe,' Debbie added.

'Yes,' I said, 'I think I understand.'

Mum's friend Pat had given my mother a brooch and a gold ring set with a large crystal stone about two years before she died. It seemed a strange thing to do because Pat was several years younger than my mother and I remember thinking at the time that it was more usual to hand down jewellery rather than hand it up. But Pat had sons rather than daughters of her own. Maybe she thought that the pieces might go to her friend's daughters after she passed? I'd hoped so, as she was like an aunt to us, and it would be natural for Mum to pass us the jewellery at some future date.

The stone in the ring looked like a large solitaire diamond and we jokingly called it the 'Elizabeth Taylor' ring. It was a ring I had coveted a lot and I occasionally borrowed it. I secretly wondered if this was the ring she meant, but I was wary of giving anything away so said nothing. My

Mum promised to leave it to me in her will, but I teased her that I would get a real diamond instead.

'Hang on, I'm getting a name now. Pat?'

Debbie and I both slumped back on the sofa in relief. It was Pat! How exciting that she'd given us a great description but then the name too. I was impressed, it wasn't as if she'd given us a whole list of names … just the one. The medium smiled and we stopped and had a mouthful of tea before she carried on.

I looked around the room. It was fairly dark and dusty in Sandra's spare room. I knew the medium had been unwell for a long time and when I looked at her now she looked frail. A twinge of guilt hit me in the stomach. Sandra had put off our appointment twice due to ill health and I remembered how anxious I'd felt for our visit, feeling a little cross inside about the inconvenience of the delay. She had a long waiting list and each cancellation meant another wait of several months.

Now as I looked around the room I wanted to search out a duster and rush around the room with it, to help her in some way. But I knew if I'd have even mentioned such a thing I would have totally offended her. The poor woman. Of course she would be offended. What did the dust matter anyway, she wasn't bothered by it so why should I be? Random thoughts flickered through my mind as I heard gentle chatter in the background. For a moment I just totally zoned out. She was talking to my sister Debbie.

Unusual objects seemed to have been left in the room.

A sweater was folded over the back of a chair and a strange newspaper cutting was propped up on the mantelpiece of what would have once been a fireplace. Also on the mantelpiece was a pair of mismatched glasses: one was a wine glass and the other a short tumbler. They seemed out of place. Had someone had a drink and left the glasses in the room? Both had been decorated with glass paints in bright reds and orange. The room was a little untidy and I guess I had wanted mystical chic.

You don't comment on other people's things unless you are going to say something nice and I couldn't think of anything to say which would have made any sense. I realized I had been staring and someone was talking to me. I turned back to face the medium and I smiled as she handed me a pack of tarot cards.

'Shuffle the cards, dear, and place eight of them on the table. No make it ten, no fifteen.'

Debbie and I looked at each other. We were excited and bemused.

'Yes that's it, place them face down on the table. Ok now turn up the first two or three.'

She began talking again and I blurred in and out. Debbie was furiously scribbling notes for me whilst the medium gave me a reading from the tarot cards. I felt that the reader was using the cards more for my benefit than her own. As I turned over each card at her request I noticed she didn't even look at them.

'I see you writing,' she said. I nodded. 'Writing a book.

In fact, although it's going to be slow at first, eventually you're going to have more work than you can handle. You're going to write a lot.'

I grinned and looked at Debbie who was trying to note it all down as fast as she could. Sandra asked me to place another ten cards face down on the table and turn over half of them. Again she didn't look at the cards.

'I do write, actually. I've just started.' I muttered.

'Good, good. Yes I can see you on TV.'

'TV? Really? Not radio?'

In my mind I'd thought that one day I'd like to go on radio and chat about my new research into angels and the afterlife, but I'd never thought I would go on television.

'Yes, radio too but TV, lots of TV. You're going to be well known.'

'I am? Cool!'

I was thrilled. Was I giving something away in my body language? But why was I pleased about going on television. Am I shallow? Did it matter?

'You'll have published your first book within eighteen months, they're telling me. Then there'll be others … lots more.'

As it happened, that book took a little longer, about two years actually, before it finally hit the shops, but whether the event was pre-ordained or I'd been encouraged to succeed by the message I'll never know.

I was desperate to know more but she asked me to pick up the cards and pass them to my sister. It was her turn now and I scribbled furiously until her turn ended, way too soon. I could see how people became addicted to this stuff! Perhaps it's the ego hearing what it wants, taking what it wants from the message. But she'd already started talking again.

'I have another lady here, on your mother's side,' she began. 'She's with someone, her husband I think, and they are showing me a horse and cart. He's making deliveries door to door.'

We both nodded again. Could this be granddad? He used to be a milkman.

'Now I'm seeing a bakery. It's connected to the lady. She's making cakes and things.'

We weren't sure but later Mum reminded us that our Nan worked for years in a bakery called 'The Home Made'. How could we have forgotten this piece of family history?

'You don't know? That's okay. Write it down, she says, and ask your Mum later. She'll tell you. The lady is showing herself surrounded by children, loads of them, and she's wearing a uniform.' She continued.

This was brilliant stuff. How could she have known? Our nan had worked in an orphanage for years and years. There were pictures at our parents' house of Nan in her uniform with her starched white apron, surrounded by forty or fifty children!

There were other relatives who came with messages that night. Brief appearances were made by friends and relatives from both sides of the family. I remember looking at my watch again. We had already been at her home for two hours and I wondered if it was time to go. Was she going to ask us to leave now?

'Do you want to have a go on the table?' she asked.

Debbie shrugged and smiled.

She beckoned us to stand up and behind her armchair was a low glass table. Stuck on the table were the letters of the alphabet spread out in a big sweep all around the edge. The table was set up to look like a ouija board, or a 'talking board'. She reached over and picked up one of the glasses from the mantel and I suddenly realized what the painted glasses were for! They hadn't just been left in the room. When I looked closer they were quite pretty. Maybe someone had made them for her as a gift? The glasses were to be our pointers, to move around the table to spell out words – messages from the other side?

Momentarily, I was nervous. Weren't these things dangerous? I had a flashback, memories of one day as a teenager. Sitting in my parents' old house, my sisters and a couple of friends and I had laid out our own felt-tip letters in a variation of what kids all over the world call 'ask the glass'. We taped the letters onto the back of an old drinks tray and ceremoniously selected one of the best sherry glasses out of the cabinet before placing our fingers on the glass to ask our first question.

As someone called out, 'Is anybody there?' the glass began to move at once and we all ran in different directions.

'Did you push that?'

'No! Of course not, you know I wouldn't do that. Swear it wasn't you! Go on, swear.'

'I didn't move it, it wasn't me. Oh my God, oh my God, do you think it was a spirit?'

'It wasn't me, really it wasn't. Swear it wasn't you!'

Someone was crying. We were all so scared that we never really got started. I remember someone suggesting that we burned the letters so that the spirits wouldn't get us. I think we probably flushed them down the toilet or something but that was the first and the last time I had done anything like that … until now.

The medium was explaining what to do and had already muttered some words of protection before placing her finger on the glass and indicating that we do the same. The four of us sat around the table and the medium began to ask questions.

What on earth were we doing? I felt like a naughty schoolgirl but of course we were not naughty – we were adults and we were doing this on purpose. I tried to calm myself down; after all, 'the medium is in charge and she must know what she is doing', I rationalized!

The glass spun over to the letter 'V' and then the letter 'I'. What was that? I felt disappointed. The medium began chatting in a very normal tone as if a neighbour had popped in to say hello.

'Is that you, Vi?'

The glass moved over to the word 'yes'.

I felt annoyed again. 'We are paying for this and she is chatting to her friends', I thought crossly, but unreasonably. I felt like a real cow. A spirit friend had crossed the dimensions to communicate and I was quibbling about who it was. Maybe this Vi would be able to hear my thoughts? She would know what I was thinking, she would know that I was a cow.

'Sorry, Vi love, I'm with clients tonight. It's lovely of you to pop in for a visit. Could you come again another night?'

The glass went back to the word 'yes' again and the medium explained about her old friend and then apologized. I figured it was not really her fault, after all. Did it even matter? What was wrong with me? Why was I thinking like this tonight? I immediately felt guilty again. Perhaps it was nerves.

'Would anyone else like to come for a chat?' she asked randomly.

The glass went to the letter 'E', then 'R', 'I' and 'C'. Debbie and I looked at each other and I noticed the tears prick her eyes.

'Eric?'

'Who's Eric, love?'

'My Dad's brother.'

Debbie was sobbing quietly now.

'Is everything okay? Are you happy to talk to Eric?'

'Yes, we're fine. Yes, yes everything is okay, she's just very happy. We both are.'

A single tear was rolling down my cheek and I brushed

it away. I was the calm one. I was fine with all of this, wasn't I? I shouldn't have been crying.

Oh my God. Was this Uncle Eric? This was the first communication since he'd died and we hardly dared believe it was true. Excitement hit the pit of my stomach and I felt both sick and slightly dizzy at the same time. We were convinced it was him but disappointingly, Sandra was not.

'Well, you must test them, love. Always check that they are who they say they are. Go on, ask a question. Ask him something like, "What did he do for a living?" Find out if it's really him.'

I didn't want to. What if it was some fake spirit trying to trick us? I wanted to believe it was my uncle. We didn't ask the question because the glass was already moving. It was spelling out a reply. SEW.

'Sew? No, that can't be right, can it?' The medium exchanged confused glances with her friend. 'Surely he means something else, he didn't sew for a living did he?'

Debbie and I both nodded before explaining that Uncle Eric did sew for a living; he was an upholsterer. I'd been trying to think of a short word which might suggest the answer, and the word which sprung to mind was upholstery. Not short exactly. Debbie was thinking of the word SOFA, but SEW was just fine too. We both started laughing in a hysterical sort of way. Sew was a good word. It gave us what we needed. He'd passed the test. It really was Eric.

We asked a lot more questions. At one point both Sandra

and Janice lifted their fingers off the glass. Debbie and I were aware that the glass continued to move even after they had done so, although it moved a little slower. We were working the glass with the spirits, Debbie and I. Maybe, just maybe, we could do this at home? Perhaps we didn't need the medium after all – can we talk to the spirits, just the two of us, any time we wanted to?

I honestly don't remember much else. We chatted some more. I think I'd reached saturation point. We'd already received so much proof and I couldn't wait to go home and tell everyone about it.

Again, I know that other relatives came through. We still have the notes somewhere. After the medium 'closed down' the communication on the table I was ready to go home, but she was ready for more. I looked at my watch and we'd now been at her house for over three hours. We'd certainly had our money's worth, and I was tired. She was so kind, wanting to make sure we were happy with our evening.

'We didn't have time to do the spirit in the mirror,' the medium said, almost disappointed.

We knew what 'spirit in the mirror meant', as our friend had told us about this after her own visit. Sandra turned out all but a small red light and we squinted at the mirror.

'Soften your eyes. Can you see anything? Is there anyone in the mirror?'

The idea was that in the half light you could often see spirit images overlay your own. It wasn't that they distorted your face so much as the spirit face seemed to float over your own. I was only half listening. This was a fascinating exercise but there was nothing left in me to give. I'd already put on my coat and my mind was 'on the way home'. We decided to call it a day … or a night.

We walked down the stairs, both of us in a slight daze. What an extraordinary night! It was one I don't think I will ever forget. I'd had paranormal experiences all of my life. I always believed there must be something else going on in the world – another world, another life, an afterlife. There was no longer any doubt. I knew there was something else, something out there, something in there.

As for Eric, this was the first of many visits. We handed over our very small fee to the medium on our way out. It seemed way too little for the time she'd spent on us. I pressed another five pound note into her hands but she refused the money. I insisted. I felt the evening was worth a lot more and eventually she took the money, but handed it over to her friend Janice.

'Thank you both. It's been a great evening.'

As we drove home we talked about the night. Was it too late to call at Mum's on the way home? It was late and we agreed we'd both go over as soon as Debbie finished work the next day. There was a lot to share, and a long list of things to check out. Our loved ones live on after they pass, and after tonight, I knew for sure.

CHAPTER 3

Going It Alone

Nothing happens unless first a dream.

Carl Sandburg

Top priority was calling my sister Dilly in Cornwall the following morning. I remember working with the list and going over every detail of what happened the night before.

'Honestly, Dill, Debbie and I were moving the glass on our own. We did it, just the two of us. I really feel we should all visit Cornwall and try this for ourselves!' I rushed on.

'I think you should all visit too. Come down and we can have a go together.'

'Are you sure? I really want to.'

'Yes, but Nick will want to join in too.'

It was agreed. The sisters would visit Cornwall and we would communicate with our deceased relatives using a spirit board we would make ourselves. Nick was my brother-in-law. Of course he should sit with the sisters whilst we made contact. We were going to his house after all! But I was concerned about my nephews, Dilly's boys.

In the back of my mind, I still thought the communication might be dangerous in some way. I remembered tales of adventurous teens who'd communicated with spirits in the way we had ... but their experiences were negative. Some of them had written to me on my website.

One girl told me the curtains in her living room were standing on end and things were thrown about the room by annoyed spirits. A teenage boy said when his friends used a spirit board the pointer spelt out that one of them would die. They were terrified and I didn't blame them. Surely we were doing something different. We'd be careful.

I felt exhausted. This was the world's most exciting discovery, wasn't it? I felt like I'd landed on the moon. Why don't more people know about this communication secret? Surely anyone with a few letters and a glass could prove the existence of an afterlife. It really did seem that simple.

Later that afternoon, in the warmth of the afternoon sun shining through the living room window, I fell asleep. My mind needed to try and assimilate the awesomeness of the experience of the day before, and when I awoke a few hours later my mind was clearer. I needed to try and do some research about the safest way to make contact using this method. Would I find anything on the internet? I felt sure there were rules we needed to follow.

Picking up my notebook and pen I began to make notes on my own, even before I'd logged onto the computer: 'clear room, light a candle, bring in the light using appropriate words, use frankincense; add pictures of angels to the table' I began. I'd no idea where my inspiration was coming from but it seemed as if I had a 'knowing' on some deep inner level. Perhaps I'd made contact in other lifetimes; I already seemed to know what we had to do.

'Stay polite, ask for specific types of communication, invite relatives, don't ask for just "anyone", INTENT.' What did I mean by that? What you give out is what you get back. If you ask for just anyone to talk to you then that is whom you are inviting … anyone. We didn't want to talk to just anyone, we wanted a spirit family 'party'. A party of loved ones who'd long since died, and we wanted to invite only them.

I could see it clearly in my mind. If you have a house party and leave the front door open, yelling for any passing folk to join in, you soon get a full house. Word spreads and people begin turning up on motorbikes and in cars with radios blaring and disturbing the neighbours. They walk into your house in large groups with packs of beer. They spill drink on your carpet and are sick down the back of your sofa. Who are 'they'? They stub out their cigarettes on your coffee table and steal your leather jacket which is hanging in the hall. Why would we invite just anyone? I understood the word INTENT. I was being given a visual image in my mind. Intent is everything.

'Write down specific words to invited people. Ask God to come, ask the angels to help. Ask them to act as "bouncers" so that only the people we invite come.'

I never did search online. I rang Debbie later, and shared my list with her.

'It's a good idea but I've got something else for you. I heard a phrase. Write down ABC.'

'What's that?'

'Angel Board Communicator.'

'Okay, I get it.' I said, and I did get it. It was important to show we were aiming to contact only the highest realms, indicating we wanted messages of love and positive intent. As soon as I put the phone down, more messages came. It wasn't a ouija board, it was an angel board.

'With the love of God, we ask our personal Guardian Spirits to act as a gateway to the spirit realms.'

I had to write this down to stick on the board.

'We ask for protection from the highest source and contact only those specified for the highest good,' I continued.

Later on I rang Dilly again.

'Don't worry,' she said. 'I know you don't have time to make anything. Tell me what you want and I'll print off the letters and things on the computer. We can stick them on the kitchen table.'

'That's great.' I felt immense relief at not having to prepare everything. 'Don't forget to print some pictures of angels. Shall I send you some?'

'No, I'm good.'

When Debbie arrived home from work we rushed round to Mum's. Debbie had already called my other sister Di to join us.

Mum took it all calmly and I suppose there is no reason why she wouldn't. We went down the list a few points at a time and Mum filled in all the blanks. There were a few things we'd been unsure of, but in a way this was much better. Now Mum was confirming things for us that we hadn't known about in advance, so we couldn't have given away any clues to either the medium or any passing spirits, and best of all, we couldn't have influenced the information that was coming through.

'Don't you remember that Nan worked at the Home Made? Aunty Marline worked there too. She worked there for years.'

On and on it went. Aunty this and great uncle that. She knew all the bits we didn't. It's funny how you forget important family information, and there were a lot of things we should have known about and hadn't. I'd seen an American psychic on TV call it 'psychic amnesia', where people will forget the names of even the closest members of their family during a psychic reading.

Satisfied with the update we planned to make the long trek from the Midlands to the West Country the following weekend. We all squeezed into Di's small car and filled the endless journey with excited chatter. We were on an adventure into the unknown.

On the first night I was ready to get started but everyone was tired. We did chat a little more about the whole phenomenon but I was disappointed. I wanted to do this now! Let's get on the angel board!

The next day was filled with girly shopping and family

fun but I was distracted and eager to start. When my nephews went to bed I fetched my bag to lay out my 'kit'. Dilly reassured me that the boys wouldn't come downstairs so I felt happy.

With no luck finding the frankincense oil I felt we needed, I placed my substitute frankincense aromatherapy candle on the side and lit it. We all sat around the kitchen table and Dilly whipped off the tablecloth to show us the ready-prepared table with letters and angels stuck on it in a circle. It was like opening an exciting present, a secret, hidden beneath the cloth. It was brilliant.

I'd already walked around the room with some incense before saying a few reassuring words. Dilly fetched a small tumbler and placed it in the middle of the table. We all looked at each other, wondering who would start, who would say the first words. I offered to read out the messages I'd written in my notebook. We needed to write down the messages as we received them so we wouldn't forget. Dilly got up from the table and returned with a pen and pad of paper.

'Okay?'

'With God's blessing, we wish to communicate with our loved ones on the other side, receiving messages of love and good intent.'

The glass moved immediately and I was aware that my cheeks felt warm with anticipation. We'd positioned the table so the pendant lamp hung low over the centre of the table, illuminating the letters clearly. The glass had already spelt out its first word.

HI.

'May we ask you your name?'

The glass spun round and round as if in excitement before spelling out its message: GUESS WHO. GUESS WHO.

'Please can you spell out your name?'

ERIC.

The glass went wild now, moving in and out, right to the edges of the board in front of each of us in turn as if someone were acknowledging us all, saying hello.

ERIC, ERIC.

'Uncle Eric?'

ERIC.

The light was flickering wildly over the table now as we all burst out laughing.

'Hi … Hello!' we all grinned.

'Do you think it's really him?' someone whispered.

'Hello, Uncle Eric!'

Everyone had tears in their eyes.

'It's real isn't it?' I said, more as confirmation than a question.

Over and over again the glass moved, one letter at a time, before BANG!

The flickering light bulb had blown over the table, and the room was plunged into near darkness. Di and Dilly gasped and Nick reached over and switched on another light, but the drinking glass continued to spin at speed around the table, still pointing to each of us in turn. We all sat wide eyed and slightly shocked before someone burst out laughing once again.

'Eric, was that you? Oh my God do you think he blew the light bulb?'

Dilly jumped up from the table and the giggling commenced.

'It's okay, I have a spare bulb, but someone has to come with me! I'm not searching in the cupboard on my own!' she laughed.

What a family reunion! Relative after relative communicated that night. We could do it! Are we all mediums in our own way? Had the spirits contacted us, reaching out across the heavens using a combination of all of our energies? How did it work and actually, did it matter?

We seemed addicted to the process and when we finally called a halt to the evening session it was well into the early hours of the morning. No one had really wanted to finish but Dilly had reminded us that, of course, we could have another go the next night.

We all joined hands and I read out my closing statement. I thanked the spirits for visiting us and asked that they consider coming back the following night, whilst we sat with them again. I also asked that the contact be ended for the night, but it didn't work quite as we'd intended. Di, Debbie and I were staying the night at Nick's parents' home and we drove the few miles down the road before letting ourselves quietly into the house.

I woke up several times, as if relatives who'd been unable

to get through were trying to visit me still. Di remembered having an out of body experience where she'd been looking down at me floating at the bottom of the stairs … luckily I didn't remember! What a weird night.

Dilly had a spirit visitor in the night too. An estranged aunt came to her during the early hours. This aunt had treated Dilly badly in life and she had clearly decided to use the opportunity to say sorry now by showing her a spirit board and spelling out the words SORRY in a sort of dream vision. We were all exhausted the following morning and exchanged notes.

Debbie remembers little except that she was ashamed of Dianne's and my sleepwear. She'd arrived as a well-seasoned visitor with a glamorous, long silky nightgown and robe. Apparently, I was wearing a pair of scruffy pyjamas and Di had brought an old t-shirt! Although we'd been assigned different bedrooms we all ended up together. No one admitted they'd been affected by the evening's experience. Like small sisters who huddle together after a nightmare we'd reverted to childhood and pulled mattresses onto the floor so that we could be together. No one had a lot of sleep.

The next night was our last. We had one more short session on our angel board, but it wasn't as satisfying as the first. Eric turned up again of course but we'd seen the show already. Relatives had gathered from far and wide but we'd already spoken with them. To be honest, that last evening was a bit of a let down. It was the day after the family reunion, and it felt like the day after Christmas. But I had to admit, it was the start of another journey and I was determined to use this new tool again. And so we returned home.

I'd barely unpacked my bag when my friend Wendy arrived the next morning for coffee. She rushed in, all excited.

'Hi Wendy, how are you?'

'Fine, thanks. I have a message for you – at least I think it's for you.'

'A message?'

'Yes, who's Eric?'

'You're kidding right?' I was shocked to say the least. 'Have you been speaking to Debbie?'

'No, why?'

'Did you know we'd been away all weekend and why? We've been to Cornwall and … no, tell me about your message first.'

'Well, it's not a message exactly but it's just this name. I've been hearing the name "Eric" all weekend, and I feel sure that I have to give you the name as a sort of confirmation of something.'

How on earth had Wendy picked up the name Eric? Of course, I brought her up to date with what we had been doing and why 'Eric' was so significant a name for me. If there had been any doubt whatsoever, then it had totally left me now. Eric had also been visiting my friend whilst we were away to ensure that we realized the whole spirit board communication was a real experience. Eric might have been a much loved uncle when he was alive, but he was determined not to be forgotten now he had 'died'.

Communicating with letters and a glass might be dangerous if used incorrectly but for us it had been a wonderful tool and an amazing way of establishing a family reunion. Of course, Wendy couldn't wait to have a go on the board with us!

CHAPTER 4

Meeting the Spirit Guides

Your own guide is in touch with you all the time Daisy … no matter how they communicate, everyone can tap into their guidance. You use it every day without even knowing it. Most of us have more than one guide. Gracious, I have a dozen …

Aunt Phoebe, in *Fireworks* by Jill Wellington and Edna Mae Holm

We'd spoken to our loved ones on the 'other side' but I had read a lot about angels and spirit guides and I wondered if it would be possible to chat with them on the angel board, too.

Spirit guides are advanced human souls, who act as our teachers and friends from the 'other side'. Our spirit guides are aware of our life path – our goals and wishes. Their role is to support this path and help to ensure we reach these goals by helping to place the right people in our lives at the right time.

I'd been reading a lot about spirit guides at this time. Not everyone has a Native American spirit guide, as so many TV shows seem to indicate, but other archetypes include religious figures and other wise figures from history. I wanted to know more about my own guide. Most people agree that we are born with our own spirit guide and that others pop in and out of our lives as special skills are needed.

If you want to learn to play the piano, then guides with musical talents will step forward. If you want to learn to paint then a guide with an interest in art will come and assist. If you want to become good at handling money then a guide with knowledge in this area will be attracted to you … you get the idea. I believe that what many people experience as 'angels' are probably their personal guides. Most of us can't tell the difference and I don't think it matters as long as the energy is positive, and 'feels' and acts in our highest interests.

When I was a child I used to see a male figure in my bedroom – I would wake up several times a night and this person was always standing in my room, but as I awoke the figure would fade away. The visitor was a spirit. Was this my guide watching over me? Was his voice the 'inner counsel' that supported my life? Was he my 'intuition' and my 'natural instinct'? Did he have a name even?

As soon as possible I decided I needed to make a portable angel board; something we could carry around rather than a bag of letters. Di, Debbie and I would get together with our friend Wendy and it could be at any of our houses, so we needed to be prepared. We had to be able to chat with our friends anywhere and at any time.

I felt that I needed to take charge of the task and raced

into town to buy a large sheet of card from our local art shop. I decided to be creative and was keen on using a gold-coloured board to make our communication instrument. To be honest, it never really worked out well. It looked great but they didn't seem to be able to see the letters. I think the gold card reflected too much. Or maybe I had just made it too complicated?

We always communicated with the 'other side' in full light – preferably daylight, but at least sitting in a room with all the lights on. I spent hours creating fancy symbols as 'short-cut' words but in the end, most of the time we just used the plain white card on the reverse side of the board which was easier for the spirits to 'see'.

Eric was good with the symbols, but most of the other spirit visitors could barely communicate for more than a few seconds anyway, due to their own difficulties with moving into our plane of existence. We made up the white side of the board with just the A–Z letters (printed from the computer in a large font) to make it simple, and the words 'yes' and 'no'. Now at least we had a choice. Longer messages with Eric on the gold side of the board, and short 'hello's and 'we love you's from other relatives on the white side.

Debbie's house was the chosen venue for the first home contact. Debbie had a spare room downstairs with a door we could close – to keep the children out. It was always funny if someone came to the door when we were working. Should we smile as they walked into the room? Should we rush and hide what we were doing? Should we close down the session, invite them in or send them away? It was always a dilemma.

Wendy was nervous as well as excited. I could see the whole experience through her eyes and remembered how in awe we had felt when presented with 'the big secret', in the early days of our contact with the heavenly realms. She hadn't been involved at all at this point and everything was new to her. Already, we felt like the experts, which is bizarre now I think about it.

We set up the room much as we had before – I had typed out a special message (a sort of prayer) to invite our loved ones and we asked that each of us be surrounded by a white light of protection. I always imagined myself surrounded by a fluffy white cloud and it made me feel safe. Our protection ritual seemed to do the trick.

By this time I had bought a bottle of frankincense oil and placed two or three drops of oil into the water at the top of my oil burner. The messages were always clearer when we used the oil but most people didn't like the smell! Still, the messages were more important so we worked with it anyway. You can get used to anything if you have to, and after a while I even started to like it. Debbie always complained but I insisted.

Naturally, Eric came through first, and then relatives and friends for all of us. Di is much younger than the rest of us and hadn't experienced the deaths of the great aunts and uncles like we had. Her first visitor was George. George was an elderly gentleman that Di used to work with and she was stunned when he contacted her through the board. He'd made an impression on her in life and so a connection was still there in death. He remained firmly in her heart and I really believe that love is the link which binds us all – it's all we need to reach out to those that we have loved and lost, and they certainly seem to be able to feel this energy that we send out and, in turn, reach back to us.

Wendy's grandma came through, as well as other relatives and friends. Sometimes Wendy asked a question in her head and it was a shock when her reply was spelt out on the board, especially when she didn't even have her finger on the glass. I think she realized fairly quickly that it was real, but it was still a shock.

It took several more sessions for us to feel comfortable and for us all to feel the experience was 'normal'. Another friend joined us shortly afterwards and the five of us often worked together. I used to pop round to my sister's and then come home and chat about it with my husband. It never seemed odd when he asked, 'Anyone interesting come for a visit tonight?' or 'How was Eric tonight?' even though Eric had been dead to his physical body for many years.

I soon began to see how widows became obsessed with spirit communication during the war years! Using a spirit board to chat with those on the other side could have its benefits too.

Eventually, after several weeks of practice everyone was ready to test out the theory of communicating with their own spiritual guides and guardian angels. Could they contact us in this way? Could angels even spell? Eric told us he was a 'spirit guide in-training', so we gave it a go.

'Eric, who have you brought through tonight, and who is the message for?' I asked formally.

The pointer moved towards my side of the table.

'Is the message for me?'

YES

KAB …

'It's okay, try again.'

KABM

'Kabm? What's that? Is Kabm my guide?'

YES

'How do I even say that?'

KABAM

'Kab-am?'

YES

'Wow! Kabam is my spirit guide, my own personal spirit guide?'

YES

So that was it! It worked! This was like receiving the first spirit communication all over again. We really could communicate and I was flushed with excitement!

'Do you have a message for me?'

X

The X, they told us, was a kiss, or a short way of saying, 'I send you love.' It became used a lot by other spirits too.

We each met our spirit guides that night. Eric helped

them communicate at first and then later they were able to work the board themselves. Kabam was usually the best, but I think that was because I usually took charge of the angel board, and Kabam was my own guide.

Over the next few weeks I asked more and more questions about my life, but strangely, nothing about his … and he didn't offer anything. Spirit guides can answer questions but can't tell us everything. They can't tell us what to do or how to do it. Sometimes they offer guidance and always loving support of our own choices. They can help us with other things if we ask the right question in the right way.

We were always polite. Our chats with our guides were like being with life-long friends. I remember when my own guide had to go away for a short while and Eric stepped in to take over. I actually cried. Now, I know that sounds silly, but I felt like a part of me was being taken away. Of course he came back a short while later (I think he was gone about three weeks). Sometimes, when they couldn't tell us what was coming up they would spell, 'it's a secret', or 'it's a surprise'. I always hated these games but I understood this was for my highest good.

Our guides' communications, like the contact from our loved ones, was real. The communication we were receiving was nothing like the scary experiences that others had with spirit boards. With each chat we needed a 'medium', one person who had the natural ability to bring through the messages; someone to keep control and act as the main channel for the information.

I discovered the reasons for my weird and paranormal experiences as a child were because I was a medium myself. One day the pointer spelled out,'Jacky you are a medium.' My sister Di was also a medium, and others in the family also had psychic and spiritual gifts like healing. It explained a lot!

Of course, it didn't always work. I remember frustration in the early days when two of us would sit down together to work the board, and nothing would happen at all. If Eric was about then we were fine. It seems this was more as a result of Eric's own advanced communication skills than our own. But we did get better. In time we began to hear messages or 'feel them' before they were spelt out on the board. But we realized that the rituals we used for protection before and after using the board were always the most important thing of all. We had to stay safe.

Many people warn of the dangers of inviting unknown and mischievous spirits into your home, and although we were careful and this had never happened to us, there came a point when we decided it was time to stop – at least using the board with the frequency we were using it. Every problem was met with a call of 'Let's contact the spirits and ask them what they think.' We were living our lives through the board rather than trying to live our lives by our own judgment.

It was a great adventure but the point had been made. The afterlife is real. Our loved ones don't die. We are supported by loving spirit guides and angels. We have to live our own lives and learn our own lessons, and although we have more help than we ever realize, ultimately we have to work things through for ourselves. It was that simple. We had to learn our own lessons through our own life experiences, both good and bad.

Would I recommend using a spirit board or angel board as a means of communication? I guess we all have to decide what is right or wrong for us, but for the shortest time, I felt we had a glimpse into another world. One that I still visit on occasions using this same 'door'.

It was time to move on to something new. How did other people experience contact from their loved ones in the afterlife? Did people believe in angels, and if so, how did they know they were real? Did angels work with children and animals, for example? The answer is yes.

I want to open up my case files for you. Thousands of stories hit my desk and most of them are completely fascinating. I never tire of hearing stories of how an angel intervened in someone's life or how an angel saved a life. Our unseen guidance can make a life and change a life. Their visits make us see the world differently. There have been times when I have lain awake at night wondering what on earth life is about. Then there have been other nights when I have stared into the darkness and wondered what life was throwing at me. Why had I explored some of the things that I had? Why did I experience the phenomenon that I had?

I've had out of body experiences, angel visits, contact

from loved ones and spontaneous past life recall ... amongst other things. But that's a whole other book!

Let's journey through some very personal and real life experiences and investigate the phenomenon a little deeper. These stories have made me laugh, and sometimes cry. But with each there is hope, joy and deep, deep love. The Beatles had it right when they sang, 'All you need is love!' Because love, as they say, is all there is ...

Part 2

CHAPTER 5

The After Death Communication Phenomenon (ADC)

That life exists beyond death, to me there is no doubt ... that science can explain the phenomenon, only time will tell.

Anon

If this sounds bizarre then I guess in a way it is. Can our loved ones contact us from a world after death? Can they communicate with us that they are alive and well, even though they are no longer part of this existence; no longer part of our world? My experience shows me that they can, and I'd like to share some amazing stories which back this up.

If you are just curious about the phenomenon, it might make you think, 'Hang on, that happened to me once.' You might be surprised! After a chat, people who originally said, 'Well I've never heard of that', often end up saying, 'Actually,

I had an experience like that once', when they understand how the phenomenon works.

Some of what you are about to read is going to sound a little farfetched and unreal but trust me, everything in this book is true and every single experience is real. Your own beliefs may well have changed just a little bit by the end of the book, as mine did by the time I had read all the stories. What was once a hope and a dream is now complete reality for me.

Amazing experiences come to me from people of all religious backgrounds, and those with no religious belief at all. Old or young, it makes no difference. Do you believe in an afterlife or not? Your level of belief does not dictate how likely you are to have an afterlife communication experience. Children have some of the most memorable experiences of the lot. They have nothing to prove at all. Age and, indeed, disability are no barriers to love.

Does this story illustrate an afterlife? This lady emailed me a story relating to close family friends of hers.

Mum's Still Here

'A very dear female friend of mine died suddenly in 2001, leaving her distraught husband and two sons who were then aged eight and five. The older son, George, had a learning disability on the autistic spectrum of disorders and needed a lot of care. George doesn't understand about road safety and other survival techniques we need in life, but even so, his communication skills are good. He was taught to "sign" before he could speak and so he actually "signs" whilst he is speaking.

'Everyone who knew the family tried to pitch in and help after my friend passed. The younger boy, David, was tearful one night and was crying at bedtime and saying he missed his mum. His gran was hugging him and trying to comfort him when his older brother, George, amazed us by saying, "Mum hasn't really gone anywhere, she talks to everyone but says they don't ever listen, and you never listen to anyone, do you?"

'Of course, David was even more upset by that! And he complained even more, "Why doesn't she talk louder then ... and why is she talking to you, and not me?"

'George calmly explained, "All you have to do is say before you go to sleep, 'Mum, I am listening and I miss you,' and you will hear her."

'Their grandmother and I were astounded as their parents were not religious (their mother had even had a humanist burial service). As far as I know, neither child knew anything about the "afterlife" and had been taught to believe that this life was all there was. But the next day, David awoke with a big smile on his face and told his gran that during the night his mum had visited him. She had hugged him while he was asleep and had sung to him.

'Well, Jacky, I have changed the names of these boys because their Dad doesn't like the idea of an afterlife. He met a nice lady and remarried recently and is happy and the boys are too.

'The boys are closer than most brothers. David says he will always look after George and make sure he crosses the road safely, and George says, "... not bloody likely!" But they do love each other and that much is clear. I think they are probably "soul mates" and destined to help each other throughout life.'

There are more amazing children's stories later in the book.

This special story really touched my heart, and I share Freddie's story in remembrance of his life, in his mother's own words.

For the Love of Freddie

'My name is Dee and I live in Kenya. I have felt compelled to write to you since reading your book *An Angel Saved My Life*. My own son died on 28 February of this year, very suddenly and unexpected; he was only twenty-two months old. His name was Freddie Musena, Musena meaning "Friend". Freddie was born here in Africa, and my husband and I were able to give Freddie all the love and sunshine that anyone could have in a lifetime.

'Freddie was born without all four limbs, in fact he didn't have one joint, hip or shoulder in his body, groin or underarms. You may remember last year little Freddie was in the British newspapers a lot, because we were trying to obtain a visa for him to come to the UK for medical treatment and assessment, and possibly even limbs in the future. Because Freddie was Kenyan like my husband, and I am British it was very difficult getting the visa. This year, a day before his second birthday he had an appointment at Queen Mary's hospital in London to be fitted with limbs, but very sadly, he never lived to make the appointment.

'Freddie came to us at the age of ten days after a children's officer came to see me. He explained that there was a baby in the hospital for his own safety. Some local people thought the baby should be killed due to his condition. In this area in particular, people are very superstitious about these things.

'The instant that I heard of Freddie I wanted him, and the very next day I called the hospital. I took a step towards this very small, limbless baby, who was lying in a bed big enough for an adult, and my first thought was, "Can I do this," and the next thought was of pure love for this beautiful child.

'I brought him home and life began for all of us! In the short time that he was with us (we officially adopted him) he showed not only the communities here, but indeed all of Kenya that there is life after disability. His, "never say never" attitude was just amazing.

'The day that he died we were on the way to the hospital with him. He was lying over my shoulder which is the place he loved to be. He somehow came right into my neck, and kissed it. I brought him down to look at him and he looked right back at me before he closed his eyes and passed away, just like that. It was so very peaceful but at the same time, a real shock, and very unexpected. That night as he lay in his cot, women from the community came round and we all sat around him. The women sang with amazing voices.

'The next day he still looked perfect, just as if he were asleep, in the way he always slept. He looked just the same and it was hard to believe that he had died because he looked so healthy. Even his colour was the same.

'From the first day that we brought Freddie home we used to place him on our veranda and he would look up and smile, sometimes getting really excited. Of course, we couldn't see anything, so we used to say he was playing with the angels, which I now feel that he firmly was. After Freddie died, over 300 people attended his funeral which showed me that he and his disability had finally been accepted by the community.

'The day after his funeral, we walked out onto the veranda. All around one of the bottom steps was a row of white feathers. At that time I knew nothing about the connection people have with white feathers and angels, in fact it was the film *Forrest Gump* I thought about, the part where the white feather floats down.

'A few days later, I woke during the night to smell the most overpowering smell of lavender. I knew Freddie was there because I'd washed him in lavender soap gel before we buried him. Then later I found confirmation in one of your books about the smell of lavender and other flowers being another sign from the angels and those on the other side.

'I have just returned from the UK where I was visiting my children there. They too were devastated over the death of their brother Freddie. While I was in the country I saw your book on a shelf and I bought it. I read it and then felt happiness, as I knew Freddie will never be alone, which was one of my great fears. I want him to still feel the love that we have for him, but I also want him never to be alone.

'We have many children here. I have an orphanage and rescue centre, a school and clinic, and Freddie liked nothing more than to play with the children. The children loved him. They also knew him as a boy who loved all nature and flowers.

'While I was in the UK my husband Sammy stayed in Kenya. One day, he took the flowers off Freddie's grave. It was raining and he didn't want them to spoil (some of them are silk). Freddie is buried very close to us under his favourite mango tree. Sammy moved the flowers at 6.30 pm but at 6 am the next day he went into the garden and was totally shocked to see the whole grave covered in fresh flowers. Sammy asked everyone if they had put flowers onto the grave, but no one knew anything about it. We are not sure if the flowers were from Freddie or the angels. Freddie's grave is only four steps from our veranda and I am sure Sammy would have heard if anyone had been outside, so it was very strange.

'Then, on another occasion, soon after his passing, we were watching television when the lights kept going on and off for maybe a second or two. The strange thing is that the TV and my computer were not affected at all, just the lights. We have many power cuts in Kenya and it is always my poor computer that suffers, except this time … nothing.

'I was sitting at my computer looking at the screen saver three nights ago. It is a picture of Freddie, a very beautiful one of him smiling his most wonderful smile. I said to him as I used to always say, "Mammy loves you, do you love your mammy?" The printer went off, then on again all on its own. Jacky, I wasn't even touching the computer, just talking to Freddie as I always do.

'My daughter in England also had a special relationship with Freddie. On Saturday she sent me a text message from her car because she felt that she needed to tell me immediately about what had just happened to her. She was driving to a road junction where she stopped and happened to look up and see what she thought was snow. In fact, coming closer was a mass of white feathers which landed on her car. I think she was in a bit of shock, but I told her it was lovely because Freddie was also looking after her.

'The week after Freddie died we went to his church mass. I carried his bib with me and it was decorated with the words "I Love My Mummy". I had placed the bib, along with his favourite t-shirt, in the zip-up side of my handbag, so that I could have them close to me in the church. After we got home, I put my bag away, leaving the t-shirt and the bib inside. The next morning I looked down at Freddie's bed (which is close to ours), and neatly folded on the bed was the bib! I still have no idea how it got there. Strangely, I still had Freddie's t-shirt in my handbag!

'I was very angry when Freddie died because he was so happy and doing so much. But now I have to believe that he was sent to us on a mission, which he completed with great success. I am so happy that God gave us Freddie, and the chance to show everyone that a child born like Freddie is a blessing, and not something to be hidden away as if he were a curse.

'Since Freddie died the Vice President of Kenya has announced that he wants a full census of all disabled people. That has never happened before. I would like to think that it's through Freddie that this has happened. I used to welcome all media including television to visit us and do updates. The whole of Kenya knew who Freddie was, and what I was trying to do to help other disabled children here.

'Freddie's last gift was to a child who we found out about just before Freddie died. It was the wonderful gift of "limbs". This baby was eight months old and was born without arms. Freddie has always had a fund for his own treatment. About three days after Freddie died I was sitting looking at his flower-covered grave when this little boy's name popped into my head. I decided there and then that Freddie's gift to this world was to ensure that at least one other child would benefit from my child's passing.

'When I was in the UK I started to make arrangements for this child to go to the UK to be assessed and given arms. I have contacted his parents, who love him and want the best for him, they are so happy. But I have made it plain that it is Freddie's gift to James, and that I am only working through Freddie and what I feel he told me he wanted to do!

'A magazine in the UK which featured Freddie's story is going to do a follow up, but this time it will include many children in England with the same problem. Because of the love of flowers Freddie had, I want all those who read and know of Freddie to get the sweetest of flowers and take them to a child who may be sick, sad or just in need of something special, and when they are given the flowers to be told that they are from a very special little boy, Freddie Musena.

'We were also on the Jeremy Kyle Show, a show that doesn't normally do stories about sick or disabled children, but this time he did. It was a great show which also resulted in the Kenyan Embassy phoning me the same day that it was broadcast, asking if there was anything that they could do to help!

'I feel that Freddie was sent on a mission, he completed that mission with great success, everyone was aware of him and of his achievements, and then when he had finished he was called back to the angels. But Jacky, never a day goes by without me wanting him, I cry every single day, at any moment in time. I have been told that time is a great healer, but for me I will never heal and never get over the loss of my baby Freddie, my heart is filled with love for him, he is every heartbeat. I think that is why I had to contact you, I've lost him but I am still looking for him to know that he is happy and safe and he's okay.

'So many unexplained things have happened since Freddie's passing but I know it's only Freddie coming to say hello. Jacky, I feel so happy that other people will know Freddie through your book.'

Freddie's love seems to easily pass from one side of life to the other, and I feel sure that it will continue to do so for the family that loved and cared for him so well during his short, but very special life.

I have never been frightened when my loved ones appeared to me personally. The experiences are wonderful, exciting – thrilling, in fact, and they are certainly memorable.

How can it be frightening when our loved ones move close to us in this exceptional way? When people share their personal stories with me, in some cases, the visits from their loved ones happened many years before. The accounts are as clear to them now as they were when they first had them. The visits seem real – and that is because I believe that they are real. Our loved ones and angels of every description are reaching out from this side and the other side.

Although now more commonly known as 'After Death Communication' (or ADC), I actually prefer to call the experiences 'After Life Communication', because I don't believe that we actually die. Of course we shed our bodies and that is another thing entirely. These stories have totally convinced me that life goes on.

Here is another story which arrived by email:

Father-in-Law's Visit

'I went over to Spain to see my mother-in-law one year in August, after her husband had passed away in May. This happened seven years ago and at that time we stayed in a friend's apartment. My father-in-law used this apartment at times during his life, when they had extra guests staying with them.

'One night we went to bed and it was a very hot night. Around the early hours of the morning I woke up. I looked at the clock at the side of the bed, and it was showing 4.10 am by the digital clock. As I looked up I saw a man on the veranda and I assumed that my husband was unable to sleep and had maybe got up for a cigarette. At first I thought nothing of it but as I sat up I noticed my husband was still asleep in the other twin bed.

'I was so shocked initially that I dug my nails into the backs of my knees just to make sure I was not dreaming … I wasn't! This figure walked through the wall on the veranda and then came back again. I could not believe my eyes when I realized it was my father-in-law.

'I did not know what to do at that point, so I just sat there and watched. He was walking just the same as he did when he was alive, and he was shuffling along as he walked. Nothing was said. He looked around and carried on walking past and then he just disappeared!

'The apartment was on the sixth floor, so no intruder could even get up that far, and I know that it was not my imagination as I had not even been thinking about him at the time.'

Spontaneous visits such as these happen a lot, although the 'visits' are more likely to occur as a result of a direct need such as immense grief, pressing problems at home or finding ourselves in great danger. Our loved ones are able to feel this emotion from their own realms and move closer to comfort us or, in some cases, to offer advice. That initial moment of surprise is almost always replaced by deep peace or relief that they are okay.

Sometimes our loved ones can be quite ingenious. Anja wrote and shared her story with me. She is Danish but lives in England now. Her English is excellent but I have just changed a few words to make it a little easier for you to read. Many of Anja's friends call her 'Angel'.

Grandad Says Goodbye ... More Than Once

'For as long as I can remember, I have been interested in the paranormal. I've always considered myself to be a spiritual person, but without any "powers". I've been aware of a few "coincidences" in my life that I've related to angels but every page I read of your book, *An Angel Saved My Life* I could more or less relate to.

'I have always believed in the afterlife without anyone telling me about it. When I grew older I realized that most of my family share the same belief but no one had ever shared their stories with each other.

'My own experience happened in April 2001 back in Denmark. My grandparents had a house in Crete, and whilst they were down there on vacation, my grandad told my gran that he felt a little ill and wanted to go for a check up at the hospital the next day with his Greek friend who also speaks Danish. There was no need for my gran to go with them. Grandad went for his check up but the doctors found nothing wrong with him. Then, on his way out of the hospital grandad just dropped dead.

'Back in Denmark at this time I was out buying food for dinner with a friend. As soon as we got out of the supermarket I said to my friend that I really fancied eating Greek food instead of what we had just bought. It was a bit stupid after we had bought all that food, but I just couldn't let the feeling go. So I decided to invite my friend to a Greek restaurant not far from where we were. I knew the waiter there because his parents were neighbours of my grandparents in Crete. We had a lovely meal and I told my friend about Crete, my grandparents, the waiter's parents, and so on.

'Halfway home from the restaurant I got a call on my mobile phone from my mum, telling me my grandad had just passed away in Crete. At first I was in complete shock but soon after I was able to smile and laugh again because I couldn't see a better, less painful way for my grandad to pass on, and at the very same moment he had been in my thoughts. It was as if he had called me next to him in that very instant and it made me feel relieved to know that he was not alone as he passed.

'Two days later another friend was visiting me in my flat, when suddenly we both felt this presence in the room with us. It wasn't scary at all. I said to my friend that it could be my grandad coming to say goodbye and make sure I told the rest of the family that he had arrived okay on the other side, since we were the strongest believers in life after death. Half a year later I visited a clairvoyant and straight away she told me that my grandad had been with her for the couple of days since I had made my appointment. "He won't stop telling stories, and he keeps telling me about his holiday in Spain just before he passed," she said! Well, for me the first part really made sense because no one loved to tell stories more than my grandad, but he hadn't been to Spain because he was in Crete when he passed! She told me how he ended his days and that he had a choice to either come back to life or go with the angels. He didn't think twice about it, and had been having such a good time that the angels had to remind him to come back and say a last goodbye. When the clairvoyant told me that happened two days after his passing I could not believe my own ears. She told me, "He came to you because he knew you would understand, and could pass on the messages to your mum and gran."

'It's one thing to know inside that your experience is real, and quite another for someone to tell you exactly the same story, when she doesn't even know you. I told my family about my appointment with the clairvoyant and that her only error was getting Spain mixed up with Crete! My gran held her breath and looked at me with big eyes before she said, "But we went on holiday to Spain. It was just a last-minute trip, a friend invited us ... and we didn't have time to call anyone so no one in the family knew!"

'Can you imagine how surprised I was? We found out that he had died because his heart had been three times the size of a normal person's heart. Usually, people with this condition would die at a young age but he was seventy years old and had run his own business for thirty years, and built his house in Denmark and on Crete himself.

'Because my gran lost her husband, I wanted to give her something to make her feel good. She had always liked the hand-made angel pin I had bought from my clairvoyant, but I didn't have time to go all the way to another town just for that, so I decided to have a look around my local shops for something else. Suddenly I felt the strongest urge to go down a street that I hadn't walked down for years. I discovered a "serenity shop" that I had never seen before. I walked in, had a look around and to my surprise they were selling my clairvoyant's hand-made angel pins.

'I told the shop owner that I just had to buy one because my gran loved my own pin. The assistant told me a lady had been in recently looking at these pins and said she had always admired her granddaughter's angel pin. She had picked one out she liked, but didn't have enough money to buy it at the time. The assistant had it put behind the desk so that the lady could come back for it. We realized right away that the lady had been my gran, so I bought the pin right away. It was the perfect gift!

'You should have seen the look on my gran's face when she opened that present. She looked like it had just dropped down from the sky and I know that my grandad had led me to the shop that day.'

These visits and afterlife intervention stories occur all over the world and cross all religious boundaries. Men, women and children of all ages have these positive paranormal experiences, but what do they mean? Why are people having these experiences now? Is it true that it is more common to have contact from the other side at this time in history? Or is it more likely that as we become more open minded, we are able to share these personal and positive contacts from the heavenly realms? These are some of the things that I shall be exploring next.

CHAPTER 6

Spiritual Electricians

Then I looked again, and I heard the singing of
thousands and millions of angels around the throne
and the living being and the elders.
Revelation 5:11

You wouldn't believe that it could be possible for spirits to interact physically with our world, but they can. Our loved ones in spirit can be very clever when they communicate with us from their own plane of existence, and use whatever they have to hand to get our attention. For some reason, they seem to be able to affect electrical and clockwork items and use this method of communication whenever they can.

Clockwork

I receive a surprising number of stories where clockwork items have been started on their own. Have you ever heard of the phenomenon where a clock or a watch stops at the exact moment of someone's death? These 'signs' from the afterlife have been around for many years. But there are more, and our loved ones are getting more and more adept at using everyday earthly objects to make their presence known.

Musical boxes and children's toys are fun signs from our loved ones, although I know the sudden playing of a music box might make one jump initially.

This music box story reached me very recently. Andrew shares his experience.

Playing the Rabbit Music Box

'Sadly, both of my parents have passed away. My father died in 2000, and my mother in 2001. I recall a few weeks after my mother had passed away that I was simply lying in my bed and wishing that she would send a sign of some sort, just to let me know that she had crossed over safely.

'"Mam," I said, "if you are there, please let me know that you are all right."

'The following night at 1.55 exactly I was feeding my baby son in the rocking chair next to my wife's bed. She was awake and we were talking. Suddenly a small wind-up music box with a rotating rabbit on it went off in my other son's bedroom. This music box hardly every worked and yet there it was, playing its sweet music all by itself, and it completed the full cycle of the tune.

'My wife then turned to me and said, "There's your mother now, letting you know that all is okay."

'Indeed it was, but I have to say it scared the living daylights out of me! I have to confess I wasn't brave enough to venture into my son's room during the performance. I can still feel goose bumps just thinking about it.

'It could have been a freak coincidence but I doubt it. The window was closed so there was no chance of a breeze setting it off. It was too high up on the window ledge for either of my sons to reach and it had been sitting there for quite some time and completely dormant. I'd like to think that it was my parents trying to contact me, and I like to think that they are happy on the other side.'

Lynda emailed me to tell me that after her brother passed her mother had a 'very real dream' one night in which her brother had appeared. Her mother called her into the room and the pair of them were discussing the dream when suddenly a music box began playing by itself in the other room! Lynda, too, believes that her brother sent the message to confirm to her mother that his appearance in 'the dream' had been real.

It seems that maybe the 'music box' phenomenon is one of the more common ways our loved ones use to show they are around.

Here is another clockwork story. This one was kindly sent to me by Mary.

Support in a Storm

'My grandma Edith passed away several years ago. One night several months after her death we were having a very bad thunderstorm (you don't know me, Jacky, but if you did you would know I am terrified of thunderstorms). As I was sitting there shaking, I said, "Grandma Edith please protect us from this storm!" Immediately, an old musical clock started playing a Christmas song. Now the music mechanism of this clock had been broken for some time and we were unable to get it fixed, but I kept it because it was cute and the time part still worked. I was amazed when it began to play.

'I felt sure it was more than a coincidence, so I said, "Grandma Edith, if this is you, please play me another song,"and right away, the clock played another tune. After that I felt safe for the rest of the night.

'Later, I shared my experience with my mother and it turned out that she had an experience with her clock doing something similar, too, and we both just knew it was my grandma saying Hi, and telling us that she was okay.

'Sadly, shortly after grandma Edith passed, my aunt Mary, her oldest daughter, died of lung cancer. Well, one night I had a very vivid dream of a beautiful strawberry-blonde, long-haired angel coming to me and saying, "Don't be sad anymore. Your grandma and aunt are in Heaven now. They're happy and doing just fine." After that I was not sad anymore because I knew they were safe.'

Heather also has a clock story.

Grandpa Hamilton

'Although I have never seen him since he passed, I have felt my grandpa's presence close by many times and I am sure he looks over my mum, my kids and me. Back in 1971 when I was only eleven, there was a gas explosion where I lived and a row of shops was demolished, resulting in twenty-two deaths. You may have heard of the Clarkston Disaster.

'My mum and aunt used to go to these shops every afternoon, get some shopping, have a coffee and head home to meet us coming back from school. They should have been sitting in the tea room (which took the full force of the blast and nobody survived to my knowledge) when the explosion occurred. For some reason, mum had a strong urge to change her routine that day and they went to the shops in the morning and so were home when the shops came down.On Christmas day recently, the family were all at my house for dinner. I have a kitchen clock based on the cartoon *South Park*. On the turn of every hour the clock is supposed to speak in the voice of one of the four main characters. Being me, I hadn't changed the battery in about three or four years because it was high up on the wall, and I kept forgetting it was there. About 1.45 pm, just as we were about to sit down and have our dinner, the clock started going mad, speaking in all four voices, jumbled up at the one time. We all heard it and we all couldn't believe that it was working after all these years. Not only that, but it was not even on the hour, and should only speak in one voice at a time. Once again, I felt Grandpa was there with us. I am sure that angels are looking out for us, or that Grandpa Hamilton is perhaps a "Guardian Angel". Thank you for writing your books. They are so uplifting and I have now invited the angels into my life. My parents are eighty-four and eighty-five and my dad is not in good health. I feel now that I am more prepared for when the time comes for them to pass over, certain in the knowledge that I will see them both again one day.'

Heather's story does show how comforting it is to receive contact from our loved ones. They seem to bring such fun with them, who could be afraid of death?

Flickering Lights

It is important that we are not frightened by our visitors so if we are looking for a sign from the 'other realms' then flickering lights are a good one, and if you remember from earlier chapters, I have much experience with flickering lights myself.

If you ask for grandma to let you know that she is okay, and then the kitchen light starts switching itself on an off, in the back of your mind you might 'wonder' if it's being caused by another reason, a logical reason. Flickering lights are less scary than some of the other things our loved ones might try. Is this paranormal or coincidence?

Audrey had a strange experience with lights, too.

Sharing the Wine

'When my husband died two years ago the family home was sold. The night before we were to hand over the keys I returned to the house to sit and reflect on the twenty-five years we'd had together.

'With the house being left empty my daughter put the lights on, so it still looked lived in. When I arrived that night the lights were all off. I thought that maybe the bulbs had blown because they had been left on for so long. I went in and tried to put the lounge light on, but it did not work, then in the kitchen the same again; the only light working was the upstairs hall.

'I decided not to bother and instead, I sat on the floor and put the gas fire on and opened a bottle of wine. I thought of all the happy times we'd shared together in the house, and played out the memories which seemed to be alive in my head at that moment. Then without warning and nothing being tampered with all the lights came on, all on their own. I was not frightened by this but felt it was my husband saying goodbye, which was really nice.'

There is a strange postscript to this story. When I started to email Audrey back, my computer mouse started playing up and flickering from one letter to another on the screen.

This is what I wrote to Audrey in my reply. 'As I sat down to reply to you, my mouse suddenly had a mind of its own. The curser started flickering all over the screen and pointed at different letters and words one at a time. It was so strange,

I called my mother in from the kitchen to come and look at the screen. As it continued for a few minutes, I wondered if it was a "message" so I grabbed my pen and notepad off the desk, and wrote down each letter in turn.

'It spelt out "THIS I MANIPULATE LADY, SURROUNDING, CHATTING, GUIDANCE, JACKY NEWCOMB. SEEMS TO ME LIKE THINGS WORK REAL OUR JACKY – FOR YOU."

'Mum and I just laughed, and not one time did I touch the keyboard. "Someone" around me has a fun sense of humour! I'm only cross I didn't realize that it was spelling out immediately ... I wonder what part of the message I had missed! It was priceless ... of course you know that "Eric" got the blame!'

Kim also had an electric light experience and told me, 'I can remember when my former husband's mother died. I went to see her body in the chapel of rest and at one stage the lights flickered. I thought she must be giving me a sign that she knew I was there.'

Have lights flickered for you when you have asked for a sign?

Computer Screens

Our loved ones in spirit have no fear of using the latest technology. A lovely lady called Debbie wrote to me with pages of mystical experiences she'd had since her husband passed over.

The Hat

One day Debbie was searching the internet for what she called 'comfort sites', when her late husband appeared on the computer screen in front of her. He was wearing the hat she'd bought for him – a hat he never wore when he was alive.

She told me, 'I had bought him a hat, a style he never wore, but I thought it would look quite charming on him … I had a bet with a friend that I could get him to wear it. Well, he never did wear it. However, that day on the computer monitor, he was wearing the hat so I won my bet eventually.'

Telephones

Our loved ones can ring us on the phone. No I am not kidding! This type of phenomenon is rare, I'll admit, but I have had several case histories where people have asked for a sign and then the telephone has rung with no one at the other end. Of course, we are able to trace back the call using 'last caller ID' now, so when it turns out that the number which rang us does not exist, we begin to wonder …

I've had this happen to me on several occasions but Sherri's story is special because she heard a voice at the end of the telephone too.

Hello from Dad

Sherri's beloved dad left his message on the family answer phone at her mother's house. Sherri could see the look of shock on her mother's face as she walked in the door. Her mother asked her to play the answering machine and listen to the message. 'I played it and almost fell off my chair. It was my dad's voice, yet Dad had died a little over a year earlier. He said my mother's name loud and clear ... "Eileen"!'

The experience followed shortly after her mother had told her that her father often called her name whilst she slept, but that he hadn't done it in a while! No one had heard the telephone ring at the time the message was left and the caller ID didn't show the call at all. But it made me wonder, do they need caller ID in heaven?

The nice thing about a recording is that you can replay the message over and over. Perhaps that was the intent in this case. Sherri and her family can hear the voice whenever they wish. Sherri told me that they managed to save the message on the machine for a very long time before it got accidentally deleted. They were quite happy though, as they had already managed to record the voice for future use.

I have written before about a similar telephone call. It was a father calling for his daughter and the father said several words, including that he was sorry he had to leave, and also asked his daughter to look after her mother. This was a normal telephone call in all respects except that the conversation was with someone who was deceased!

The conversation took place during the daytime, and there were other family members in the room at the time the conversation was taking place. Strangely, just before the phone rang, the gentleman concerned had been the subject of the conversation. Maybe this is our loved ones' preferred communication method for the future! As in the case above, no number was recorded on the telephone.

Imagine if you could telephone them back. Or that they could ring us every week to see how we were getting on. 'Hello, this is heaven calling!' Who knows what the future might bring.

Ruth wrote to share her story about her nan.

Nan Calling

'We recently lost my beloved Nan on 8 January this year. I was extremely close to my Nan, having spent a great deal of time with her over the years. Although I have an older brother and four other cousins, my relationship with Nan was just a little bit special.

'As you can imagine there are loads of things I miss, but one of the main things is her regular phone calls. Each evening at 6 pm sharp the phone would ring. We never chatted long and the conversation always ran the same: how was work, how are the children ... you can imagine! But it was our routine and it was familiar and comfortable.

'No matter how ill she was she would always ring just for a quick chat. I always used to feel a little bit useless as she would often confide how much pain she was in. She had chronic arthritis for years, and I would often say, "Keep taking the medicine, Nan." wishing that I could do more.

'Recently I had a very strange experience. In the early hours of Saturday morning I had to get up with my baby son. Once he was finally settled back in his cot and asleep I returned to bed. I felt that I was drifting off to sleep, all warm and cosy. Then I felt as though I was sort of dreaming, but I heard the phone ring and I answered it. I know it sounds mad – I felt and saw myself move through the house and there I stood with the phone in my hand. You probably know whose voice it was! As I spoke there was disbelief, this couldn't be her, I couldn't be hearing her voice! I heard my Nan so clearly, "Hello Ruth, I'm all right, I'm not in pain, I don't need the medicine anymore." She also said she loved us and she would watch the children always. I am still a little confused at how I felt I was in my bed, and watched myself move through the house at the same time.

'As soon as I woke in the morning, I asked my husband if he had heard the phone ring in the night, or if I had got out of bed during the night. He hadn't but he is quite a believer in the afterlife so was very encouraging.

'I would really like to believe that my Nan has tried to contact me. So many times I said I wish I could hear her voice one more time.'

Mobiles (cell phones) are also used by the other side. Our loved ones like to keep up to date with the latest technology. This story is from Sam.

'An Angel' Called My Mobile

'After my father's death, my uncle, who also had cancer, gave up. Shortly after my dad's funeral my uncle died too. We had to go to Wales to bury him and then the following weekend we went to Glastonbury to bury my dad's ashes in the Chalice Well Gardens. It's been a trying time.

'While we were away in Wales for my uncle's funeral, my sister had a strange "dream". It was on the third night of our stay and she said the whole family was gathered round in the living room (where my uncle had died and we were actually sleeping in the room on the night of her "dream"). Our cousin Rhiannon's mobile phone started ringing. It then clicked onto answer machine so that everyone could hear, as if it were on a loud speaker. And my uncle said, "I'm just phoning to let you know I arrived safely," and then my sister woke up.

'My cousins explained how my uncle was always one for making people ring when they got back home after visiting so he knew they had arrived safely.'

I've noticed that many of the dream-type experiences involve the 'dreamer' waking up almost immediately after their experience. Of course this makes it easier to remember the whole thing, so I'm sure it's no coincidence at all. I love the way our relatives stick to their familiar routines once they reach the other side, which is extremely reassuring.

Music

When my daughter was ill as a child, I heard the amazing sound of a celestial choir. The angels sounded exactly the way you might expect, with perfectly harmonized harp and voice melodies. Sometimes people hear the angels sing when they cross over to the other side and even when babies are born.

As I mentioned earlier, our loved ones like to keep up to date, and are happy to play more familiar tunes to announce their arrival.

Brigitte heard music – twice!

Song from Dad

'In March 2000 my father passed away and I took comfort from my belief in the next world, and of course angels! In fact I asked the angelic realm for support during this difficult time.

'During the autumn of 2002 I was standing at the kitchen sink washing up. I was thinking of my father and wondering what the next world is really like and hoping he was happy there. My husband was taking that afternoon off so that we could visit my father's grave which is several miles away. Suddenly I realized that repeated line "It's all too beautiful" from the old song "Itchycoo Park" was playing in my head quite clearly. I put it down to my imagination, just thinking that it's what I wanted to believe! But the angels, if indeed it was them, did not stop there!

'An hour or so later we travelled to the cemetery and as usual parked only a few feet in front of my father's grave. We spent thirty minutes or so tidying up and putting fresh flowers in the vase, and when the time came for us to leave and collect the children from school I became tearful. We got back into the car and as I was looking towards the grave, when my husband decided to switch on the radio to lighten the mood a little. Can you imagine how amazed I was as I stared bleary-eyed at my father's grave? The words being sung at that moment were "It's all too beautiful"! Well it certainly helped me to dry my tears and I find it impossible to believe that it was only a coincidence.'

Did you notice that word again? 'Coincidence?' It makes you think doesn't it.

CHAPTER 7

Dream Visitations

... And when he came to me, as if in a dream,
I immediately knew that there was more to life than this.

Anon

If you ever have a dream visitation – a visit from a deceased loved one, who appears to you when you are 'asleep' – you will instantly recognize the experience as more than a dream. People say to me, 'But it seemed so real.' The visiting spirits seem to be able to access the human mind during dream state. These 'dream' visitations are nothing like a normal dream. We actually take part in the action and can ask questions and receive answers as if we were actually aware and awake ... which of course, in a way, we are. We've already seen a few of these, so let's explore it a little more.

So how do they do this?

Simple Dream Visitation Creation

Our spirit friends can jump into a dream 'in progress'

(if it's remotely suitable and logical), or with a bit of help from spirits 'in the know', they can create a dream scene especially for us. Many of these 'dreams' are set in a plain room with only two chairs (one for you, and one for your spirit visitor), so that the two of you appear to be having a normal conversation in a standard, if not slightly bare room.

In other cases you can be joined by living relatives who appear to be 'waiting their turn' for a chat. They (our spirit friends) can occasionally arrange for several relatives to be gathered together, in a dream state, to talk to the deceased loved one, one at a time.

Pagan and visionary artist Neil Geddes-Ward had an experience in a more familiar setting.

Meet Me in the Bar

'I had a "dream" of my late friend. When he appeared to me, I was so taken aback that I woke up. I was a little upset of course, at not being able to stay asleep. So I asked to have another dream of him if I fell asleep again, which I did. This time I was in a room with him, and I was leaning against a bar, and as I turned round he was smiling at me.

'I asked him, "Are we in the Astral Plane?" and he said, "Not exactly." I asked him if he was all right and he said, "Yes," and with that, the dream faded.

'I've had other dreams of him where he is taking part as a viewer in my dreams, watching it unfold. In these dreams I looked across at him and he just winked at me. I knew he was contacting me from another level of reality. We both spoke about "channelling", creating reality and life after death. It was the main topic of our conversations.'

I'm not suggesting that creating 'dream incubation' is an easy thing for a spirit to do; however, it is one of the most common types of spirit communication. When we sleep, the ego self is out of the way. We accept things that we would normally find difficult to deal with in waking reality. How hard would it be for a solid version of a lost love to suddenly appear at breakfast!

A death of a loved one is the most difficult and painful experience for a human to endure. We believe that our loved ones are lost to us forever, but it seems that they are not … at least not totally.

Symbolism

We live on a different 'vibration' to our spirit friends. Imagine an ice cube – water in its frozen state. Heat it up and it melts. Warm it to boiling point and it turns to steam. So we have water, in three different states – but all still water. Our loved ones in the afterlife seem like water vapour to us but in their own realms they have form and structure.

There is still so much we do not understand about the way our life and our Universe work. When Einstein produced his theories of relativity it changed the way we thought about space and time. Quantum physics has taken over and modern physics struggles constantly to explain life as we know it. But at the time of writing this book it seems that even the humble 'string theory' might be in trouble. Electron bubbles, atoms, black holes ... this exploration confuses most of us! It might be many years before science and physics are able to explain these phenomena, assuming we can understand the explanation!

I once had a dream which seemed to explain the process of communication in a way I felt I understood. In this dream, I found myself in a helicopter, and my role was to pass messages to people who were climbing a very high mountain. These letters from family and friends could be dropped off at base camps at various points up the mountain. The climbers loved to hear news about their loved ones at home, but passing messages back down the mountain was even harder than sending post up the mountain.

Carrying paper and pens up a mountain was just an extra weight, but they were happy to give me messages verbally which I passed back with pleasure. The messages were simple like, 'Thank you for your letter, I love you very much', and 'Tell Julie, congratulations on the new baby.'

Sometimes, when an urgent message needed passing on, I was able to jot down a few notes, picking up more details to relay to the folks back home, and at other times, the climbers were able to write a few short letters for me to pass on for them. When they climbed back down the mountain, some of them were able to telephone from the call box in the local town, but the connection wasn't always clear up on the mountain!

I woke up feeling as if I had been given a simple explanation about how our spirit friends try to communicate with us – it seemed to make a lot of sense to me at the time. Communication from this different level of reality is not without its problems, as you can see.

It is possible to send and receive information through these vast distances of space and time, but the messages need to be simple and easy to understand. Even with a great deal of experience on the part of the sender and the receiver, messages are not always received clearly. Phone boxes can be broken, weather conditions might not allow communication to take place, sometimes there is a crackle on the line or the line even goes dead ... well, you get the idea.

Let's look at some of the dream visitation symbolism more closely.

The Closed Gate to Heaven

When visiting loved ones in dreams, many people see a barrier that they are not allowed to cross. A meeting takes place with your loved one but we cannot go through the 'barrier' that they have come through to enable them to visit us. This barrier is a visual indication of the difference between their realm and ours and might be represented by a wall, a stream or maybe a gate. They can visit us, but usually, we have to stay on our side. Would 'crossing over' mean death or a near death experience?

Millions of people all over the world have had a near death experience. A near death experience, or NDE, is where the spiritual body leaves the physical body at the point of physical death. With the dramatic progress in medical science, many more people are being brought back from the very brink of death. Not everyone has a memory of the experience but millions of people do go through near death and come back to life with a tale to tell of their journey to the other side.

At this time of near death, classic experiences include the spirit of the person being pulled away and upwards from the physical body and being drawn towards a white light. Usually we are met by a being of light, familiar guides or angels, or loved ones on the other side who come to collect us. In most cases we reach a kind of barrier here too, or gateway (the fabled 'Pearly Gates'). It is at this point that we are usually turned back and told it is not our time. We are then sent back into the physical body to continue life in the human realm.

This barrier, in all its different forms, is what we often see in a dream visitation. We can be aware that there is an obstruction or boundary that we are not permitted to pass. Once we cross through the barrier, this would usually mean physical death (but not always as we will see later). Sometimes we are taken for a short visit to these other realms.

Valerie was shown in no uncertain terms to stay her side of the line!

No Entry

'My grandad had passed away six years prior to my dream. I was chasing him, but no matter how fast I ran I couldn't catch him, even though he was walking with a stick! When I eventually caught up to him, he walked through a doorway and the door slammed in my face!'

In Valerie's case, the doorway that her granddad walked through was the barrier. We'll see more of these barrier stories later.

Sometimes our loved ones will bring us a life message. Nick was visited on three separate occasions by Ted, a close family friend who had passed over some time before. The first dream was a bit of an introduction to the phenomenon.

Nick says, 'As a child, Ted was one of those people we called "Uncle", even though he wasn't actually related. Our relationship was very close … closer than a relative even, and in my formative years, he was always around.' Nick realized that his dream experience was a real visitation. Here is his story.

Don't Take Life So Seriously

'It was only a couple of weeks after he died when he first came to me in a dream. I knew immediately that this wasn't an ordinary dream. I felt him touch me and when I discussed the dream with his wife, she told me that she'd had similar dream experiences herself since he'd passed. Ted told his wife that it takes a lot of energy to communicate in "dream state".

'In the first dream, I was lying down and he just came and looked at me and said, "Don't worry about me I'm absolutely fine." He put my hand on his beard. The beard was part of how we identified him, that and his sandals and his pipe! It was a reassurance, a way of knowing it was really him. I could actually feel the spikes of his beard, it was amazing! The dream is still as fresh now as it was then!'

Later, Ted visited Nick again ...

'Ted's daughter Sarah (a close friend) and I were in a multi-storey car park, just chatting. Ted appeared, and his dad Norman was in the background too. Both were dressed in white ... they appeared to be fizzing with energy. I felt that their energy was like that of a sixteen year old, and their vitality was shimmering out of them. This time he didn't say anything. He just looked at me, and I felt that they were on their way to an important mission, and were just passing through. In the dream, I felt as if my friend Sarah was aware of the presence of her father and grandfather, but she didn't see them as I did.'

The next time, Nick was prepared.

'The third dream was in late August. It was in a very stressful time in my life, when Ted appeared to me in a vision of our old house. His wife and daughter (both still alive) were in the room too. We were sitting in the lounge, when I said to him, "You know you're dead, don't you?" and he said, "Of course I do!"

'I asked him, "What do you do now you're dead?" and he told me it was fantastic in the place where he is now. He told me how he could do anything he wants to – and spends a lot of time flying! He said that we forget that when we are on the Earth we take everything so seriously, and don't laugh enough. He started messing around to prove his point, and just started bouncing and jumping around the lounge! His message was that we should enjoy life whilst we can.

'When I woke up, I felt brilliant. This time he had given me a definite message. We were killing ourselves laughing in this dream and I actually woke up crying with laughter!'

Nick obviously took this message to heart and now works as the very successful humorous, spiritual writer and columnist, 'Cornish Writer'!

Holding the Vision in the 'Middle Realms' – The Visitors' Room

These dream visitations are usually fairly short as the spirits explain themselves; it is very draining holding their energy together in this way. It is only with practice and regular visits that our loved ones improve and manage to stay around a little longer … like Eric.

Andy's grandfather was keen to tell him about the spirit realms too, but seemed to run out of time. Are spirits restricted to the length of time they can visit? I doubt it, I'm convinced that it's more to do with the length of time they can hold themselves in the lower vibration which is required to create the contact.

Never Enough Time to Chat

'I had never lost anyone close to me, and my grandfather was more like a father. We were extremely close. My grandparents lost their first son, Andy, aged five. My grandfather has always believed that I am his reincarnated son, and I was named Andy after my uncle.

'For many years before my grandfather's death, we would talk about how he might communicate with me after his passing.

'I have seen my grandfather in dreams several times since his death. In one dream I actually had a short conversation with him. In the dream, I was at my grandparents' house, my grandmother and aunt (both still alive) were present in the dream. Then my grandfather appeared. I was very happy to see him, but I was a bit distraught that it had been many months since his last contact. I asked him if he is aware of the things I do in my daily life. He answered, "Yes, but it doesn't work the way you are thinking."

'My grandfather had a sad, almost annoyed look on his face. It seemed as if he was frustrated that he couldn't stay longer and explain to me how things work in his new home. Then he left my dream. I do remember that my aunt and grandmother were sort of facing away from my grandfather and me. After my grandfather left, I remember turning to my grandmother and asking her if she had seen what had happened. She sort of shrugged her shoulders as if unaware that my grandfather had been with us.'

I remember watching the American psychic medium John Edward talking about the way he communicates with the spirits in the afterlife, and he said it was a little like they were in the bottom of a deep swimming pool, which in essence is very close to us and we can dive in and visit them if we want to but it is hard to hold our breath for any length of time. They are so close but we cannot keep ourselves at the bottom of the pool for long. With practice we could hold our breath for longer and so 'visit' them for longer. I feel that when our loved ones visit us it is a similar phenomenon … only in reverse.

There is much scientific proof that we leave our physical bodies every night when we dream. Our spirit temporarily leaves the body to visit the astral realms – the place of dreams. When we sleep, our spiritual body rises in 'vibration' and lifts up into these places. Our loved ones in spirit can move down to meet us for short periods of time – a kind of 'halfway house'.

A psychic medium (a psychic who communicates with the 'dead') works in a similar way. A medium doesn't have to sleep to reach this higher vibration. A natural medium is born with this ability already but many people can train themselves to 'tune in' to a certain extent. Visiting spirits, in turn, temporarily lower their vibration to make a short-term communication. A dream is an easier way to do this as we are already in a different state of consciousness than our normal waking selves.

Wendy told me about how difficult it was to come to terms with her father's death until he visited her three months after he had died. Her experience was similar to the first one that I had myself, in that she found herself in a simply furnished room.

Accepting a Loss

'I remember walking into a room which appeared to have a pink haze. Dad was sitting in a straight-backed chair in the middle of the room – nothing else was in the room. Dad asked me why I kept crying, and how could he help me to go on.

'I cannot remember my reply, but I just know from that day forward I no longer sobbed myself to sleep. Although I still miss him, I began to accept my loss after he visited me.'

Wendy's experience had a purpose, and it was to comfort her and help her to move forward in her grief.

Creating a dream space where we'll feel comfortable in meeting our loved ones is also a common scenario. It does not have to be a room with just two chairs. Sometimes props are added.

Patty's grandfather was a regular communicator and enjoyed making the visit into a social occasion.

Evenings Out

'My grandfather often visits me in my dreams. In my dreams we're usually sitting drinking tea or playing billiards (he taught me to play) and we talk about what we're each doing in our separate existences (I never remember his, but it seems to have something to do with school, or studying but I don't know what) and he always has good advice for whatever I'm doing. This has happened about six times since his death, and is very comforting.

'I have a friend whose grandmother visits her whenever she has problems; only in her case they sit around a campfire (her grandmother was part Native American).'

Have you experienced a visit like this one? Have your loved ones told you what it's like on the other side?

What's it Like on the Other Side?

Sometimes our spirit friends will discuss heaven itself. I know that my own school friend and I had a really in-depth conversation (and that I asked a lot of questions about what he does and where he is), but I really couldn't remember that part of the conversation at all afterwards. Maybe it wasn't important. Or perhaps we receive information on a 'need-to-know' basis only. I guess at that time I just didn't need to know.

Abigail's friend Bruce died when they were both about 13. Abigail, like me, also asked a lot of questions but she also didn't remember the answers.

Chatting about Heaven

'Bruce and I had been such good friends. But a year or so passed after his death, and I quit thinking of him. In fact, I never thought of Bruce again.

'Then suddenly he came to see me one night in my bedroom. He was dressed in a long white gown, and he literally "lit up" the room with a beautiful white light. I felt such peace and calmness in his presence. I cannot describe my feelings so that anyone could understand. All my sadness left, and I felt so free and peaceful.

'He spoke to me about Heaven and other things, and I was so entranced with what he told me. My spirit understood every word, but the weird thing is ... if you asked me what he said specifically, I couldn't tell you. His message was for my spirit, not for the human part of me to understand. I know that he talked to me for the longest time, while I said not a word.

'At the end of our visit, Bruce drifted upward. As he began to fade from sight, I begged him to come back and tell me more about Heaven. But he just smiled at me and faded away.'

I believe we remember as much as we are able to understand at the time. I realized with my own experiences that I learnt more as time went on, and perhaps I was able to accept their message and incorporate it into my own reality.

A spirit's message is to comfort us, and to let us know they are alive and well. When our loved ones cross over, all becomes very clear indeed. On death the spirit remembers that our physical life is just a school for the learning spirit – something we, who have been left behind, have completely forgotten.

Spirits usually show themselves in ways we might recognize them. They usually appear well, healthy and whole, even if they didn't appear that way in death. Health problems which affected them as living human beings seem to have disappeared once they crossed over.

The spirit can take on any form, or none at all. This seems to be a question of personal choice, and is also dependent on their knowledge of how this might be done. Usually they show themselves in the 'body' of their previous life; the life in which we have so recently lost them. Sometimes they appear as a bright light.

This story is special in that it helps a loved one with closure. Beverly had an experience which involved her father. Her family was devastated when he passed so abruptly. Her 'dream' seemed to explain it all.

Speedy Passing ... for Love

'We were all back at home and going through his terminal illness again, however this time it was much worse. In the dream the cancer had spread to his brain and he was very much out of character, violent and abusive, it was a horrible dream.

'When the dream finished my dad said, "And that's what could have happened, that's why I had to go so quickly."

'For years I had been angry that I hadn't been there at the end and now, let's just say it's made me think ...'

Visitors with Spirit Guides

Not all of our loved ones visit alone. Sometimes a new spirit is accompanied by a spiritual guide (the same spiritual teachers and friend that helped us on this side of life) or even an angel.The spirit guide is often seen in the background,and particularly with the newly deceased and with children who are nearly always accompanied by a guide or another relative.

Jackie was troubled after her young son had suffered a lot of painful medical procedures before he died. She needed to know that Jerry was safe and being looked after on the other side. Jerry appeared with his escort to show that he was safe and well.

Okay Now Mama

'After Jerry died, these events haunted me. I couldn't sleep and when I did, I had nightmares about what my baby had endured before he died. Then one night I woke to find two figures standing in the doorway of my bedroom ... an adult and a child.

I immediately knew that it was Jerry and his "protector". They had no features, just two white shapes. I blinked a couple of times but they were still there.

'Then I heard (in my head) Jerry say, "Mama, don't worry about me anymore. I'm all right..." and with that they were gone. I feel that God allowed Jerry to visit me so that he could bring me the peace I so needed. And it worked ... I haven't had a nightmare concerning Jerry since then.'

Jackie's story really illustrates the power of what these visitations are all about. Debbie had a similar experience in which guides also appeared alongside loved ones. Debbie had been lucky enough to have had similar experiences before.

Family Visit

'Around six months after my husband's death, I had a minor accident one morning, while taking my dogs to the vets. I hit a deer with the car which really frightened me. Needless to say, I was very upset and took the day off work to recover. I came home and went to bed in tears.

'Eventually I fell asleep, but while I was sleeping, my husband came to me in a dream visitation. It was wonderful but my husband also brought me some spirit helpers. Just before the dream ended, he also brought my son from a previous marriage, who had passed away twenty years before. I had never had a dream visit from that child and I was just ecstatic.'

In this next story, a relative is the escort. Was Grandma looking after this little boy?

Grandma Babysitter

'I had given birth at twenty-eight weeks to twin boys, Michael and Jamie. Michael was the smallest baby out of the two at 2lb but he was the strongest. Jamie came in at 3lb 1oz but never opened his eyes. When I lost Jamie I thought the pain would never go away. It was a really hard time.

'Just before their sixth birthday I was in bed fast asleep and I thought I was having a wonderful dream, I felt myself being raised off my bed and there was a mist in front of me. A very bright light was coming from the centre of the mist, which then began to clear. First I saw Jamie as he would have been aged six with my nan who had died twenty years before. She had her hand on his shoulder. Then I noticed that there was a different hand on Jamie's other shoulder ... also on my nan's shoulder, but I could not see the face of the other person.

'Jamie and my nan just stood there smiling at me and I heard in my head that they were okay and I was not to cry anymore. I felt nothing but the most powerful feeling of love and after a while they seemed to go backwards into the mist and I felt myself thrown back onto my bed.

'My husband woke up with the jolt I had caused and he asked me what was wrong. I told him what had happened and he held me and cried, and said I was the luckiest woman in the world and that it was not a dream.'

I agree that this was not a dream. It bears every similarity to the other visitation experiences we have read so far. When this lady shared her story with her own mother, she suggested that the figure standing behind her nan was probably her grandfather who had died when she was only two years old.

Our loved ones can appear in dream visitations to bring us messages about children who might be born into the family in the future. The children (or babies) seem to be in a spiritual waiting area with our loved ones, and waiting to be birthed.

They can also bring us important information about the conditions of the birth, like Maria's story which we'll read about next.

Maria's Grandma Brings a Special Message

'In 1980 after ten months of marriage I looked at the end of my bed, and saw my grandma who had died when I was a child in 1964. She was holding a baby. Then grandma spoke to me and she asked me if I liked the baby, and I said yes. She then asked me if I wanted the baby and I told her that I did. I looked at my husband who was still fast asleep, and she said to me, if you don't have this baby now, you will never have a baby.

'She went and I woke my husband up, but didn't tell him what I'd seen! After that, all I could think about was having a baby. I had a baby girl a year later in 1981, but sadly my marriage broke up after that and we divorced in 1984.

'I married and divorced again after that, but didn't have another child. My daughter is now almost twenty-two years old, and several relationships later, I never did have another child. So gran was right!'

How Our Loved Ones Appear to Us

Spirits regularly appear younger than the age at which they passed. Adults often show themselves at age thirty or so, or in their prime of life. Children and babies seem to 'grow up' in the spirit realms, and appear in visions and dreams at the age they would have been if they had lived (although I feel this might be for our benefit).

My sister Debbie told me about the day her friend Ann came to visit her in a dream (see Ann's story in Part 2, Chapter 8). Debbie said, 'Her hair was longer ... like it was when I first met her.' This does seem to be typical.

Donata's mother took on a younger profile in her visitation dream too, and looked well and happy. She told me, 'My mother seemed much younger than I can remember her; she was washing bright red apples and placing them in a blue china bowl. She then offered the bowl to me. That's the dream – for me, it was actually my mother letting me know she loved me.'

Virginia wrote to me from Canada. She had many dreams about her close friend after she passed over, and her friend made an appearance as a younger version of herself ... complete with a new (old) hairstyle!

Real and Healthy

'About two months after her passing, I dreamt that I was walking down this beautiful, pure white hallway. It was a long hallway with lots of curves. At the end of the hallway was the most beautiful flight of stairs you have ever seen. It was clean as clean could be. I remember that clearly, because I couldn't understand that ... no speck of dirt! The stairway I think was made of marble. I can't really remember if there were people, but if so, there were very few and I didn't talk to anyone ... yes, I do remember people, but they just kept walking, not in flashy clothes, just in normal everyday clothes.

'It was peaceful and I didn't fear anything. But, when I turned one of the corners, I saw my friend and she was coming towards me. She looked so real and healthy.

'I've had a couple dreams like this before, and she just looks at me with her beautiful eyes. I even had a dream of her with her hair permed. I have never known her to do this, and she looked like she was in her thirties or forties. I asked her husband if she'd ever permed her hair and he said yes, around the age of thirty-five.

'I have asked her for guidance in my work, because she was always there for me. She was my angel on earth. I am not sure now if she is trying to tell me something, but no words ever come from her. Now I am starting to realize these dreams aren't my imagination!'

Rosemary dreamed about her grandfather about two years after he died. In this dream the visitor appears in the body of a young man. He brings a message of reassurance with him as we've learnt our loved ones often do.

Grandfather Brings a Message

'I was in the sitting room at my grandmother's house with my grandmother and another elderly lady whom I did not recognize. The second lady was sitting in what has always been my grandfather's chair, and proceeded to take a small bottle of gin from a workbag beside her and take a nip while my grandmother's back was turned, giving me a huge wink in the process. My grandmother did not seem to notice all this was going on or even seem to be able to see this other person.

'My grandmother then said to me, "Vic [my grandfather] will be here in a moment ... look, there he comes." At this point I looked out of the window of the sitting room and saw a dark-haired young man (who I instinctively knew was my grandfather, although his hair had gone white while he was very young). He walked down the path which is next to the house but promptly disappeared as he reached the gate next to the sitting room window.

'At this point I woke up with a very strong message in my head to tell my mother, "Don't worry, we are looking after Ruth" (my grandmother, who is still alive). In the morning I told my mother what had happened and fortunately she is open to such things, and she said that the second lady, whom I hadn't recognized, sounded like my great grandma Thomas (my grandfather's mother) who died before I was born.'

Again, one of my own visitation experiences mirrors this phenomenon. I had a recent visitation where a family friend appeared to me as she had looked as a younger woman, with jet black hair.

Strangely, I had forgotten she'd even looked this way! In my own visitation I had recognized the visitor immediately and, like in earlier cases, had realized that it was not a dream, because I've had several visitations. I was aware that my friend was really visiting me after she had died.

In her later life, her once-dyed black hair had faded to a silvery grey and this is how I'd remembered her. Yet she visited me in 'her prime' – perhaps in the way in which she wished to be remembered.

Here is Carole's story.

My Lovely Young Mam

'I've just recently lost my mother. She had been poorly all of her life and she ended up with emphysema. She fought this so hard, then four years ago she was told that she had bowel cancer, which she eventually died of. I'm not really dwelling on this as she was seventy-three and, when you weigh up the problems she had, I think this is fantastic.

'The thing is, when I went to bed on the same day that she passed away, I'd just closed my eyes when I saw my mam looking a lot younger, maybe about eighteen, and she had lovely black hair. She was wearing something white and although I only got a portrait view, it was like someone was shining a torch through her garment it was so bright, and I have to say I have never seen a picture of my mam looking like this. I've been through her photo collection and there are none, as she had very few pictures of herself as a child or teenager.

'I am convinced it was my mam wanting me to see her as she is now and letting me know that she's all right.'

Saying Sorry

Occasionally, our spirit friends will come back to let us know that whatever disagreements we had in life are no longer valid after death. If we fall out with a loved one before they die, or have a silly argument, we can feel guilty because we haven't had a chance to make amends, or have missed the opportunity to say goodbye.

After death these things are not important to our passed over loved ones. The visiting spirit wants to explain this so that we can move on in our lives.

Malcolm took the opportunity to visit his friend Neil in a dream.

Still Friends

'I had a visitation last night. I was in a big room with lots of other people I knew and worked with. Malcolm and I used to work together and the two of us were friends, but in the past we'd had a big row. Although we got over it I felt guilty about it after he had died. He told me in the dream to forget it, and that it didn't matter any more. I had been thinking about it over the last couple of days so it made sense that he would say that to me. It was great because he took me back to a time when we had been better friends – I remembered it clearly after he showed it to me again in the dream.

'He became very frail just before he died and he showed himself initially to me as he was when he was very ill. It was sad because he momentarily appeared naked and very thin. Later he looked as he was when he was well again.

'Before he died, I'd found out that he was seriously ill one day when out walking in some nearby woods with my family. I'd bumped into a colleague who explained the illness to me. Amazingly, Malcolm took me to this very same place in the dream! It was as if he was trying to "set the scene" and help to remind me of who he was.'

Again, the intent of this visitation was to help Neil to 'carry on' with his earthly life. Our loved ones seem to have the ability to pick up our stronger thoughts and feelings which relate to them, even from the afterlife. Friends as well as family have this special link with us.

Do Our Visitors Always Talk to Us?

Sometimes our spirit visitors do not communicate with us at all. Maybe they can't, or perhaps they do not know what to say. In these instances, it is difficult to determine whether our visitors have arrived for our benefit or their own.

Don had no real belief in the continuation of life at the time his wife died, but said he was intrigued by his own spiritual visit.

Just Watching

'I woke up on several occasions and I know I saw my wife at the end of the bed. She was just there in the bedroom although she didn't say anything or try to communicate with me. It was as if she was watching me sleeping. I didn't know what to make of it really. It's strange, isn't it?'

Sometimes I feel our loved ones pop back to set their own minds at rest, especially if spirit passes over quickly. Perhaps by returning for a brief visitation or so it helps them to realize that their life here is over … at least for now.

Dream Witnesses

Shelagh's story is rare in that several people had a visit from the same person on the same night and all remembered it afterwards.

Shelagh had a difficult time during her pregnancy. She became pregnant shortly before the death of her dad and called out to him many times whilst she was ill in hospital. The doctors suspected she was losing the baby and Shelagh also had problems with breathing. The lady in the next bed suggested that it might be something to do with the flowers in the room – but Shelagh had never suffered from hay fever in the past. Nevertheless, she decided to have the flowers removed and by the next morning Shelagh was breathing normally.

Shelagh explained that because of the breathing problems, the doctors tried a different treatment which helped her recovery. Shelagh continues the story.

Grandfather Helps with the Safe Arrival of His Granddaughter

'They found a cervical polyp to be the source of both the bleeding and the tissue that led the first doctor to believe I was miscarrying. The following spring I gave birth to my namesake, Shelagh, the second of my three daughters, a young woman with a mission in this life. Her grandfather helped ensure her safe arrival.'

Shelagh says that she didn't understand this until over a year later when her father visited her in a dream. The really strange thing was that she wasn't the only one to receive a dream that night!

'The explanation came in a dream that I, my mother, and both of my brothers had on the same night. My mother and one brother confirmed the dream the next day; it took my remaining brother nearly ten years to admit to it.

'We were standing in a place similar to the inside of a large teepee whose function was to provide a sense of closeness and privacy. My father stood before me; to my left, eyes closed, stood my mother, and to my right, also with their eyes closed, stood my brothers. It seemed to me that my mother had already had her "turn" to speak with my father, and that my brothers would follow me.

'Dad explained that it was difficult to bring us all together in this manner, and that he couldn't maintain such a connection for long. Then he asked me if I had anything I wanted to ask him. I certainly did. "Where were you," I demanded, "the night I thought I was going to lose Shelagh? I needed you so much. I called to you and I cried myself dry. Where were you?"

'"I was there all along," Dad told me. "Remember the flowers that made you so sick? Flowers never made you sick before, they don't make you sick now and they will never make you sick again. I did that. Whenever you need me, I'll be there."'

Shelagh's father had somehow managed to manipulate the flower 'allergy' so that doctors would pick up a more complicated and dangerous problem relating to the birth.

This power to intervene in such a positive way is extremely reassuring and comforting.

Shelagh also had a spiritual visit from her mother years later. She described it as being in a half waking and half sleeping state. Her mother's message from spirit is a familiar one, and I loved it! It reminded me of Nick's story earlier in the chapter, whose 'uncle' explained what a great time he was having in the afterlife.

This story shows how much of our earthly personality is able to survive once we cross over.

We Can Do What We Want Here

'Mom has been back to visit several times, but her first visit after passing was the most memorable. She popped in, wearing a royal-blue turtle-neck sweater and looking otherwise as she did when she passed ten days earlier.

'Assessing her new surroundings, she told me, "They have classes here, but you don't have to go if you don't want to. It's not like they send you to detention ... they don't even have detention." Then she added with approval, "You can do whatever the hell you want here!"'

Priceless! What fun that the spirit retains so much of the earthly personality.

Asking for a Sign

Kathy's bereavement was very new when she wrote to me in great distress. Her story is especially painful as it is so soon after her loss. It was kind of her to allow me to use her story here in the hope of helping others. Her boyfriend Steven's visitations did comfort her a little.

Ghost

'Steven was the one true love of my life. I believe Steven has tried to comfort me by telling me to buy the movie *Ghost* so that I can better understand what happened to him.

'Then I went on the subway and a man was playing the flute to the song "Unchained Melody" from the movie *Ghost*. I also felt Steven wrap his warm presence around me a few days after I buried him.'

I wanted so badly to comfort Kathy after her loss but a loved one is no longer around to hug us in a normal physical way. It takes time to accept that we still have a life to live and that our loved ones are around – although only in a spiritual way.

I shared with Kathy some of the amazing stories that I have included in this book; stories I have received from people around the world, in the hope that she would be comforted by them.

Kathy was kind enough to write back to me the following day and tell me about the experience that followed.

'Yesterday when I wrote to you I was in really bad condition, as you know. I felt like I was going crazy. After I wrote to you I said a prayer that God would allow Steven to visit every once in a while to comfort me, and last night he did again. I felt his presence lying right next to me and it helped me through the night.'

What a fantastic story. Once again it shows that our loved ones are aware of our thoughts and feelings relating to them.

Kathy was no stranger to the visitation experience and also told me about a similar experience in the week that she lost her sister.

Sister Says Hello

'I was sleeping with my son in my bed when all of a sudden it became extremely cold in the room, so cold that I thought maybe I had left a window open. I got up to look around the apartment but there was nothing, and the rest of the apartment was warm. I went to lay back down again when I felt the mattress sink in as if someone had sat down, and when I looked up I could see it was my sister Damaris. It still gives me the chills to this day.

'She was so beautiful and radiant and all I wanted was to hear her say, "I love you" one more time. She told me, "I love you, Kali" (she always called me that – ever since she was a baby she never could pronounce Kathy) and then she left.

'I didn't want her to leave but the next morning I found out why she had to leave. You see, my family doesn't believe in angels or spirits or the afterlife. The next day I spoke with my father, and I asked him once again if he believed in angels and to my surprise he said, "I didn't but now I do, because last night I was very tired at my job and went to sleep on a bench. All of a sudden it grew really cold and I felt a chill go up my leg. I looked towards my leg and there she was, so beautiful, your sister. She told me, 'I love you, daddy, and I will always be with you.'"

'I began to cry and he said, "Kathy, what is the matter?" and then I shared with him what happened to me.'

The coldness felt with these experiences is common to ghost-hunt phenomena. Ghost hunters often look for a 'cold spot' when searching for ghosts or spirits. Scientific instruments can actually measure this drop in temperature.

Here is another temperature-drop story, sent to me from Vikki in Wales.

I Never Felt Cold Like That

'In February 2001 my mum passed away with pancreatic cancer at the age of sixty-five. She had so much faith in the afterlife that she showed little fear at all, which many would find very strange. We spoke very openly about it as my faith is also strong.

'Before she got very sick I asked her if she would try and visit me from the other side and she told me she would. Jokingly, I asked her not to appear at the end of my bed at night or else I would probably join her. We giggled together and came to the decision that she would appear in a dream.

'Sadly, after a very laboured passing she slipped away. Being the baby of the family with a five year old and a two year old it affected me badly, as I used to see her every single day, and then suddenly there was nothing.

'I was very miserable and it really affected my husband and

children as they didn't know how to ease the pain. Every night I would go to sleep and pray that tonight would be the night that my best friend and mother would come to me. Night after night passed by with rivers of tears, but I had no dreams.

'Roughly nine months passed and the tears fell a little less often, until one day I actually went through the day not thinking of her once. I felt a little sad but also pleased that maybe I was healing.

'My husband was a painter at the time and he had landed a job in England which would take him away for the weekend. I settled the children, then went to bed myself. At 3 am I began to feel her presence, I felt her hand on my cheek and her calm voice saying, "Victoria, it's me."

'My heart pounded out of my chest, tears rolled down my cheeks and I stuttered the words, "I love you so much," over and over again like a stuck record. She laughed softly and told me to calm down and that she already knew this. The feeling I had was like suffocating, like when someone is invading your personal space. If it wasn't my mum that was present I would have screamed for them to get off me as it did feel that close. But it was my mum so I would never have done that.

'At this stage I know I was very much awake but too scared to open my eyes. This seems silly as I know my mum would never hurt me, but it was the impossible and the unbelievable happening ... right there in my bedroom.

'From across the hall I heard my five year old wake and call out for me. I said to my mum that I would have to see to her because if I didn't, she would not go back off to sleep. (My daughter is a very light sleeper.) My mum agreed.

'It was at this point that I shot up from bed and walked through where I imagined she was sitting or kneeling. I have never felt cold like that before, it chilled right into my bones. As I stepped into my daughter's bedroom I felt the atmosphere warming. I settled my daughter and returned to the room. The room was also now very warm but I'm ashamed to say, I was way too afraid to return to bed!

'Since then a few other things have happened but nothing so real as that night. I guess I'm being greedy and I really should think myself lucky that it happened at all, but I am still always wishing it would happen again, and I know I won't be so afraid next time. If she comes again I would have so many questions for her.

'My family all think that it is my imagination but I know it was real.'

The Spirit Lives On

Spirits are keen to tell us that the soul doesn't die. Moving into our spiritual selves is a returning to our natural state. It's like shedding our clothes.

Let's continue with Kathy's story. Kathy's sister appeared to her again, many years later in another dream.

No Longer Dead

'I had a dream that I was getting ready to attend the funeral of my uncle Tony, who had already passed. My family kept rushing me and telling me, "You have to attend Uncle Tony's funeral," and I said, "I know but I have to go to the hospital first to visit with Damaris."

'When I arrived at the hospital two orderlies dressed in white greeted me and said, "It's a miracle, your sister is no longer dead, and she's been resurrected, awake." So I walked into the room and there she was awake, looking so beautiful, dressed in a light blue gown, not as she was when she passed at the age of fifteen, but how she would look now as an older woman. She smiled at me and then I woke up.'

I love this final visitation that Kathy had with her boyfriend Steven.

Passing Cars

'I dreamt that he was in the back seat of a car, and I was in a different car, but also in the back. We were on the road going in the opposite directions when we spotted each other. I grew frantic but he motioned that he was okay and for me to keep going. I know that he wants me to continue with our plans for me to finish college and raise my son Eli.

'I love Steven dearly and will never forget him.'

This again shows how our loved ones want us to carry on with our lives. Finishing our earthly plans is very important. Sometimes our loved ones will even indicate that they left because it was their time. They are keen to point out that we can't join them, that we must live out our lives as planned before birth. It is wonderful how they take the time to visit and show us that they are still watching and loving us.

Missing the Signs

Alison was very distressed when she first wrote to me, and rightly so. She had lost her two young nephews in a fire – a terrible tragedy. She explained to me that on behalf of her sister she had visited many mediums to try and receive a message for the grieving family, but all to no avail.

'Why,' she asked me, 'do they not "come through"?' I couldn't explain to her why and tried to comfort her with other stories that I had about contact from the other side as I did with Kathy. I do know that sometimes, when our loved ones die suddenly, or in a violent way, that they go through a time of healing and nurturing on the other side before they are ready to meet with us. Perhaps, I offered, that was the reason.

We exchanged a couple of emails before Alison happened to mention the dreams she had been having. I was stunned!

'I've had lots of dreams about them, and the feelings are so wonderful that I don't want to wake up. I am always kissing and hugging them. I suppose that is their way of contacting me!'

Yes indeed! I wanted to validate the importance of these visits and explain to Alison that her nephews were already contacting her. Visiting a medium is like someone else passing messages via the phone – why do that when they can come to visit you directly?

How many times do we miss the obvious because we are expecting something else? We have preconceived ideas about when and how this contact might take place when in fact it has been going on the whole time!

We need to pay attention to the subtle signs – or in this case, a very big sign indeed. Visiting a medium can be wonderful and comforting but if our loved ones can come through then it means we don't have to find someone who can take that call for us!

Bringing Comfort

Beverley also sent me an email with her story. Her tale was a comforting one and very simple indeed.

Don't Worry

'I still lived at home with Mum after Dad died. I was eighteen years old. I went to bed as usual and settled down to sleep and it was then that I had my experience. I can't really remember how long it was after Dad died but I don't think it was that long.

'All I remember really now is that my dad came into the bedroom accompanied by my friend who was a sort of cousin, who had died two years earlier aged just fifteen. They stood beside my bed and told me that I hadn't to worry or be upset any more, because they were all right. I remember the feeling of peace and joy surrounding them and wasn't scared at all; just comforted.'

Bringing Healing

Kevin Williams, author of *Nothing Better Than Death*, felt he was actually healed by his mother 'in spirit'. Here he explains in his own words.

Mom Heals

'When my Mom was killed on November 24, 2001, I had difficulty feeling sorrow at first because I knew that my Mom was in complete paradise. Even when my Dad broke the news to me about my Mom being killed in a car accident, my feeling was, "Wow, that's bad for me; but, it is a tremendous blessing for my Mom."

'I have for a long time believed that death was merely a door we pass through to get to an absolute nirvana, a heaven beyond our wildest imagination. However, her passing was kind of ironic because, at the time, I was in the middle of writing my "near-death" book.

'After her death, I would pray a lot that my Mom would appear to me in an "after-death communication" or a dream, as I read happens to so many people.

'At the funeral, the song "Moon River" was sung which really touched us all because it was one of her favourite songs. It was especially wonderful for me, because I hadn't heard that song since I was a child when my Mom would play it a lot.

'One night, as I ached from coughing hysterically from a week-long case of bronchitis, I was in my room resting and watching television. Suddenly, out of nowhere, the most incredible thing happened to me. It was as if a bolt of lightning hit my chest but it didn't knock me down and it didn't hurt. The bolt of lightning could also be described as a gigantic beam of unbelievable love hitting my heart.

'When it hit me, I immediately experienced an ecstasy that I have never experienced before. My back arched in pleasure and I grabbed my chest in ecstasy. The beam hit my heart and spread out over my entire body and it transformed me. I felt like a man of stone coming alive. I was in complete amazement. I didn't see the beam, but I most certainly felt it. Then, in the ecstasy of it all, I felt the powerful presence of my Mom and Jesus entering the room.

'I rejoiced in this and I kept thinking, "Thank you God, thank you Mom." The love, joy, and peace I felt, was not of this world. I basked in this love for a length of time … I don't know how long.

'But, after a while, the ecstasy subsided and I thought that was the end of the experience. By now, I was down to earth but still walking on a cloud. Soon, I felt the desire to massage my aching ribs brought on by the bronchitis. As I started to rub my chest, the ecstasy returned. Then, I came to the astounding realization that my Mom was healing me. I felt like she was "possessing" my arms and hands as I was massaging my chest. It was a strange sensation to have your arms and hands not be your own. I don't remember how long this continued, but it was a substantial amount of time. When the experience subsided and I no longer felt my Mom's presence, I went to bed. It occurred to me that nobody would ever believe me if I told them about this experience.

'When I awoke the next day, I immediately began thinking about my experience. Getting out of bed, I turned on the television and began to get dressed, all the while thinking about the experience. Then almost immediately, another event happened that would blow my mind. On television, a movie was playing a beautiful rendition of the song, "Moon River". It was the song my Mom loved so much and was sung at her funeral. It was an absolutely perfect validation that my experience was not just in my head. It was a profound revelation. In utter amazement, I began wondering what the probability would be for this to happen. How many movies have the song "Moon River" playing in it? I figured it must not be very many. Then I wondered what the probability would be that such a movie would play at exactly that date, time and channel, for me to hear it. I figured it was mathematically extremely improbable that such an event would happen.

'That day, my bronchitis began to subside and go away. I will cherish this experience for the rest of my life.'

Lyn's brother seemed to reach out to her from the other

side with a diagnosis which could well have saved her life. I have never seen these warnings myself, but of course, there are many types of allergy and maybe this was one which affected both Lyn and her brother. We'll probably never know.

Coffee Hazard

'Peter my half-brother and I always cared deeply for each other right from our childhood onwards. For a long time we never knew we were brother and sister, as this was kept from us by the adults in our family because of their own agendas.

'Sadly, Peter died at the age of thirty from cancer of the liver but he never went very far.

'Ten years later I suddenly became ill and doctors could not diagnose the cause. At that time, my husband Ken used to make me a cup of decaffeinated coffee every evening and we thought nothing of it. Three mornings in a row at the same time, Peter appeared to me in my dreams and said, "It's the coffee, Lynette!"

'Then I saw a large steaming coffee pot and a poured-out cup of very inviting coffee and then saw Peter miming to me his own illness.

'On the very first night I had that first dream, Ken told me later, as we compared notes, that he had gone to the cupboard to get the decaffeinated coffee and something stopped his hand from reaching for it. He could not get the decaffeinated coffee out and so he went and made tea for me for those three nights of the warning. I said nothing about the change in his habit, and I didn't discuss the dream with Ken until after the third appearance of Peter.

'We took the warning to mean there was something in the decaffeinated coffee that would kill me the same as Peter, so neither of us would drink any coffee after that.

'A very short time later we heard a warning in the media that said decaffeinated coffee was suspected to cause cancer!

'Peter has contacted me since in dreams, telling me things he felt I should know, bringing me touching gifts such as a single rose whose fragrant perfume I could actually smell. Since I have been given the spiritual gift of the astral traveller in my latter years [Lyn is able to have out of body experiences], I have met him, not in dreams but wide awake in the Astral realms, where I have seen him sailing a small yacht and where we have spoken on the sea shore about things that were hidden from both of us when he was on earth, but which we both know the truth of now.

'There is nothing to halt Peter from travelling between two worlds now and he does. He is a spiritual man of two dimensions.'

Although the spirit personality stays much the same after we pass on, our loved ones do seem to have some insight into our health and well-being, and sometimes can see a little way ahead in our lives.

Of course, our relatives and friends on the other side

can't tell us what to do, but only advise us in the same way they might have done on this side of life.

Helping to Get our Life Back on Track

Another reason our loved ones come to visit is to help us get our lives back on track. Mourning is a natural process but sometimes our loved ones want to bring us through the process a little quicker. Tanya had a spiritual telling off – but not in a nasty way!

What's All This About?

'On the day of my father-in-law's funeral, I went to bed obviously exhausted and very upset. I woke in the night to find my father-in-law sitting on the bed saying, "What's all this about, Tarnie (his pet name for me)?" He said it in a "come on, don't be a silly girl" voice. I had assumed at the time that I was dreaming, but somehow I doubt it.'

Tracey had the dream visitation that she'd longed for from her nan. She needed to know her grandmother was still around.

Watching Over You

'My nan died of cancer sixteen years ago, she was fifty-four. I was only ten at the time, and from the day she died, she's never been out of my thoughts.

'I'd often wished for a sign that she is around me when one night I had a dream that I was sitting on the floor in my house with my family round me (my children and my husband),when this figure walked through the living room door. The figure was transparent and as it came closer it became more solid. I was shocked to see that the figure was my nan!

'She held her hand out to pull me up from the floor. And she put her arms around me and whispered in my ear, "I do watch over you," and she reassured me that she still loves me. I woke up with tears in my eyes.'

Moving On

When our loved ones die in difficult circumstances the shock alone makes moving on particularly difficult.We get stuck within our own grief and the death scenario plays over and over again in our minds.Sometimes the reassurance that they are still around is enough to move us on emotionally.

Maria's father died in August 1998, aged seventy-two.

Please Don't Cry

'He had been ill for a long time, but had a stroke while in hospital for something else. When I got there he was unconscious. I didn't know if he could hear me, but I was the last one who saw him. I was distraught.

'Exactly twelve hours later, I had a dream where I was looking at him in his hospital bed, and I said, "Dad wake up, please wake up." A halo of fire lit up around his head and he woke up. He was very healthy and looked twenty years younger than he did when he died.

'He said to me, "Maria please don't cry, can't you see I am happy now?" When I looked at him he smiled and the halo of fire blew out like a candle. I woke up feeling warm, like I had been covered in a glow, probably a hug. I felt so happy and I feel this was his way of saying goodbye to me.'

Kate wrote to me after she had seen an article I had written about spirit visitation in *Prediction* magazine.

Feeling Grandma's Love

'My grandma died five years ago, Jacky. About a year later I was going through a tough time. I was deeply asleep one night when I heard someone say my name very clearly! I opened my eyes and noticed that the clock was dead on midnight.

'I could feel my grandma's love fill me and surround me really intensely. I felt so calm and loved, a deeper kind than I've ever experienced before. I couldn't move for the whole time and it must have lasted for an hour before it gradually faded away. I then fell into a very deep sleep.

'Other things also happened to indicate that she was around me. My watch stopped at 02.37 am, which was the time she passed away, and I also had a visit from her in a dream. In the dream I was walking down my grandma's street with two guides or angels who were walking either side of me and were dressed in black. They made me feel safe and protected. The angels walked me to grandma's garden gate and disappeared.

'As I walked up the path she appeared at the front door, and hugged me for a long time. I could feel her love but it was stronger and more intense than any love I had felt before. Then she then took me round each room of the house. It was exactly as I remembered it with the pictures and ornaments. After some time we returned to the front door and hugged in the same way as before, and I walked down the path to where my two guides were waiting for me. I felt so much better about everything from then on.'

In a lot of the stories I receive, people see their loved ones accompanied by angels or spirit guides. This story is nice because it shows how Kate is escorted by her own guides, which she might not otherwise get the opportunity to 'see' in her normal waking life.

Psychic Thoughts

Psychic mediums don't usually hear their spirit messages with their physical ears, the information usually comes from within their minds. Crickett learnt how to listen to his own grandpa's spirit.

Grandpa's Thoughts

'When I was around fourteen years old my grandpa, who had raised me, passed away and my grandma couldn't bring herself to sleep in their room, so she moved into a downstairs bedroom, and I slept in her room. From the start I knew I wasn't alone in that room. I was drawn into the room with a warm, caring sensation.

'As I was drifting off to sleep I would sense my grandpa in the room and I had conversations with him. What I mean by this is not that I heard his voice but somehow I knew what he was saying. I used to think I had to really hear the spirits, with my physical ears, but what I have learned is these thoughts come to me – thoughts that I knew were not my thoughts. It took some time before I figured out it was the spirits. This was their way of speaking to me.'

Sometimes our loved ones manage several visits to reassure and comfort us. Jane saw her father immediately after death, but he also visited many times in dreams as well as in other ways.

Dad Watching Over Me

'My father passed from cancer nine years ago when I was twenty-three. I was holding his hand as he passed. Since his passing I feel that we have a closer relationship than we ever did before, he can now reach me on a different level. He has given me the strength to sort out problems in my life and we are closer now than we had ever been in his lifetime.

'When Dad was very sick, shortly before he passed, I could tell by his face that he was seeing something so wonderful and was so in awe. Whatever he could see was so, so beautiful that I felt privileged to have been able to share that precious moment with him and to witness the look of wonder on his face. It was an experience he shared with me and I shall never forget it.

'Shortly after my dad passed he came to me in my dreams (strong, powerful dreams, quite unlike any others I have ever experienced).

'Although he passed at home, he did spend a lot of time in hospital receiving chemotherapy. In my dream I was going to the hospital to see him and was hurrying because his doctor had called me to say that the end wouldn't be long now. As I arrived outside the building, I looked up and saw Dad waving to me. He was wearing his usual outdoor coat, watching and waving from his hospital room window. I felt a sense of relief; he was going to be all right.

'When I got into the hospital, however, I was told that I was too late and that he had already passed, so he was all right because he was going to be safe on the other side and was just saying goodbye. Since then, Dad has visited me many times in my dreams (although none of the other dreams has been as strong as this one). I am always aware that he's had cancer and has passed, and the overwhelming feeling that comes to me is that I feel happy because we have come out the other side of the whole ordeal of cancer and are still "together".

'As well as seeing Dad, I have heard him. One day I was in my bedroom with my dog Scrumpy and we had the door shut. We were in the house on our own when I heard footsteps coming up the stairs. I looked at Scrumpy and he was looking at the door listening, too (he had his head on one side – like he always does when he is listening intently to something). If he heard it also, then it couldn't have been my imagination. I stared at the door handle wondering if the door would open, but the footsteps disappeared into the bathroom. It was the same time of day that Dad always had a shave. I think he was doing what he always had done at the time he had always done it.

'Another time, my mum and I were in the lounge when, rather strangely, the radio came on in the kitchen, just in time for the news, which Dad listened to every day.

'I have felt him touching me. I was up a ladder decorating and I could feel hands steadying me as I was about to topple over.

'I know Dad is here protecting me as he had always done. Fathers and daughters always have a special relationship and a love which could never die. When I was little he used to tell me, "However old you get, you will always be my little girl," and I know from my experiences that he is still here now looking out for me, protecting me.'

What a wonderful story. As we have seen, sometimes, the afterlife communication experiences make people feel even closer to their loved ones than they did in life. Julia's story is similar … and another light flickerer.

Closer Than When He Was Alive

'My dear father died three years ago, and although he was very ill at the end and it was a relief that he passed, we missed him terribly. As my family gathered at my mother's house after the funeral we were talking about a friend whose husband blinked the lights after he died. Suddenly, one of the lamps in the room began to flutter! The room hushed then we all broke into laughter, for we knew it was Dad. This happened again when we shared dinner at my sister's house.

'Back at my home after the funeral, I talked to my dad all the time, knowing he must be near. One day, I decided to write him a letter on the computer to see if he would communicate. The overhead light began to flicker and tears sprang to my eyes. I knew he was in the room with me reading my letter.

'I continued to do this for several months, and he would blink the light. I felt closer to him at that time than when he was alive because we had lived three hundred miles apart and I rarely saw him. Now he was right in the room with me all the time, reading my letters. I shared with him many memories and thanked him for being a wonderful father.

'After about three months, I felt at peace knowing he was still "alive" and with me. I no longer felt the need to write to him and the flickering lights ended. If I need him, I still talk to him and know that he is listening.'

Just the simplest of appearances is sometimes all that we need. Julie's parents tragically died when she was seventeen, but their visit was a great comfort to her.

> 'Approximately six months after their death, they both appeared to me, neither spoke or touched me but it was a message that everything would be okay.'

Faye's grandparents just popped over for a brief visit but it made all the difference to Faye. Did Simon's grandparents look after him whilst he was in a coma?

He'll Be Okay

> 'My cousin was in a terrible car accident and was in a coma for about six weeks. I had a dream that I was walking through a park with my nan, grandad and my cousin Simon, and they said, "Look, Faye, we told you he'd be okay."
>
> 'Days later my cousin woke from his coma, and whilst he's not in 100 per cent perfect health, five years on he's alive and well, and working abroad now as a chef!'

'Dream visitation' appears to be the most common form of spirit visitation. Have you had a strange experience yourself? I bet you have. It's surprisingly common and we usually file it away in the 'wasn't that a strange dream' drawer in our minds.

Are these dream visitations real visits from the other side? I believe they are but, ultimately, you have to make up your own mind. They make us feel safe and loved, they bring healing and happiness. Dream visitations are one of the gentlest and easiest ways for our loved ones to visit us, but spirits are capable of a lot more than dream visitation as we will see next.

CHAPTER 8

Announcing Visitations

I felt him gently brush my cheek and look at me longingly, yet as I awoke his image faded away ... he'd come to say goodbye and it was the last time I saw him.

Anon

Our loved ones on the other side often 'hang around' waiting for other family members from this side of life, when it is their time. They are waiting to collect us, and escort us over. Sometimes these interactions occur when we are ill, in accidents or at moments of great stress and need.

I worked with a lady whose husband was dying of cancer. As his time drew near he appeared to have a foot in 'both camps'. He was confined to bed and every day, as my friend left for work, his spiritual adventures would begin. Each evening, he told her how he had spent the day floating out of his body, and visiting old childhood haunts. He seemed to have become very fluid within his physical body, and would tell her, 'Mum came to see me today', or 'I've been out with mum while you were at work.' But his mother was already on the other side.

It's easy to write this off as the delusions of a dying man but is it possible that this reality had some merit in the real world? I believe that it did but my friend was unsure. But of course, I have the benefit of thousands of other similar case histories as reference.

The dying often see and hear both realms. My grandmother, for example, chatted to her husband and son in spirit, in the days before she passed. She was longing to be with them again and seemed to have the ability to see and hear them clearly. But my grandmother was not the only one. Medical personnel and care workers who spend time with the dying recount similar situations. It's very common, although perhaps not commonly talked about ... yet.

A family friend lost his wife last year. He has to take special medication to control his Parkinson's disease and each time he takes a certain drug he sees his dead wife for a few days afterwards. The drug has a side-effect – it makes him clairvoyant (which literally means 'clear-seeing'). He can see his wife at these times but I can't help wondering if she is with him ALL the time anyway. This particular family friend has visited me personally in dreams too.

Sometimes our own souls have the ability to communicate with loved ones before we leave for the spirit realms, and in other cases, at the very moment of death. Even more bizarrely, soul-to-soul communication has occurred even when a person is not dying, but is unable to communicate in any other, normal way.

World-renowned angel teacher Diana Cooper shared a special memory with me.

I'm Still Me Inside

'The most dramatic memory I have of someone coming to me was my mother. She had not passed over but was senile. She came to me in the form I had known her when I was a child. She looked young, beautiful and glowing, and her eyes were filled with such love. It was incredible and made me feel enfolded in love. I have treasured that memory. My mother's still alive, so she wasn't announcing her death. It was a few years ago. I think her higher self was asking me to see her from a different perspective.'

Our loved ones can also let us know that they have passed. People experience a wide range of emotions including feelings of great peace and love. Sometimes a voice is heard but at other times it is just a deep inner 'knowing' that our loved ones have gone.

Steve's mother had been seriously ill in hospital in the UK. It was a tragic situation. She was just fifty years old and dying of cancer. There was nothing left to do and so Steve decided to drive his family from Plymouth to Burton-on-Trent, a distance of many hours' drive.

Goodbye

'I remember when I left the hospital that Sunday to make the journey home, looking back at her and the strangest feeling coming over me. I couldn't put a description on the feeling, just that there was something there. Three days later I was at work and I got a call from my brother telling me to get home quickly as this was it, mum was going to pass.

'I jumped into the car, picked up the family and set off for Burton. I drove up the motorway as fast as the car would possibly go, undertaking and overtaking like a man possessed. When we got onto the A roads I continued the same, overtaking at the slightest chance in the hope that I would get there in time.

'Then all of a sudden I felt a great calm around me, a peace ... I don't know how else to describe it. There was a feeling on my shoulder, not a physical force as such, although I feel that there was a hand there on my shoulder telling me to slow down, there was no rush as it was too late.

'I slowed down and my wife asked me why, so I told her. She made a note of the time. When we got to the hospital we were, in fact, too late as I had suspected. The thing that makes me convinced that it was my mother was the fact that she had come to me to make me slow down, to protect me and my family.

'The recorded time of death was precisely the time my wife had noted in the car.

'Was it my mother? I like to think that it was. Was she coming to say goodbye to me because I couldn't get to her? I'll always think of it that way.'

Although Steve and the family did not make it to his mother's bedside before she passed, she was still with them as she crossed over.

Beverly wrote to me with this personal account.

Thank You

'A couple of years ago I looked after a lady who was terminally ill at home. I was her main nurse and we became very close (I am a community nurse).

'One night I was woken up with a vivid image of this lady, and when I sat up in bed I thought I had been woken up by a dream, but when I looked at the clock I somehow knew that she had died. I felt that she had come to say goodbye and thank you.

'At work the next day it was confirmed by my colleague that she had died at the time I had been woken up.'

Here is another 'announcing dream'. This is how Keith's grandmother announced her impending passing.

Going Soon

'My grandmother was dying. She had a history of leukaemia and strokes over the past few years and would not let go. The night she died my father was at the nursing home, practically begging her to let go, telling her that everyone would be all right and it was her time. He reminded her that Grandad was waiting for her, and anything else he could think to say. He still thinks that she was afraid to die, and in a way that was true.

'I had a visit from her that night ... "before" she died. She came to me in spirit. I believe she was trying to check on all the loved ones she had before she left. I could see that she was having trouble letting go because she didn't think my father or I could make it without her. I told her that we would all be fine and that it was hard for us to see her in such pain. We would all miss her, but could take care of ourselves and would feel better that she had passed on to her rest.

'She stayed a few minutes and I felt she was trying to reassure herself that I would be okay, and then she left. Later that night she "shook off her cloak" and passed on.'

Nicole was just a small girl when her nana came to say goodbye. By visiting personally in this special way she would certainly have eased the pain of her passing.

Going on a Journey

'When I was five, Nana was diagnosed with breast cancer. I was very close to her and didn't understand what people meant when they said she was sick. One night I had a dream. In my dream my next-door neighbour rang the doorbell and I ran to answer it. He said, "Hi Nicole, I have a special visitor for you, but you have to be quick as she has a long journey to make." All of a sudden he turned into my nana. She said, "Nicole, I love you and I always will. Just make sure you remember that, okay? I will be your guardian angel for life." I said, "Nana, I love you too." Then she said, "I have to go now, but we will meet again some day."

The next morning I ran down to mammy and daddy and they said, "Nicole, we have something to tell you." I stopped them and said, "I already know, she died last night." They were absolutely astounded and asked how I knew so I told them how she had visited me in the night.'

Cathy heard from an old school friend.

Last Call

'On 31 December 2004 I heard the name of a boy that I went to school with, whilst I was sleeping. I also heard the word soul.

'When I got up I went to the supermarket to get food in for the New Year and I thought that I would probably bump into Roy at the shop but I didn't. Then two days later my younger sister phoned to tell me that Roy had died very suddenly of cancer. He had been ill for six weeks and died minutes after the New Year in an ambulance.'

It is possible to experience a physical touch on occasion. Debbie's mother was still in a coma (from which she never woke up), when she felt her mother kiss her goodbye.

Goodbye Kiss

'I lay down in my bed to go to sleep. Something floated down from the ceiling and kissed me on the forehead. It was transparent but I could see it ... kind of like a mist. I don't know why, but I thought it was my mother.

'I was awake when this happened. I got up and called the nursing home my mother was in because I was sure she had passed away. She hadn't passed away but she'd had another stroke. She died three days later.'

This next experience happened around the time of passing. Jerdana's visitation was very shortly after the death of her grandmother.

Sorry for the Way I Treated You

'My adopted mother's mother had never really accepted me into the family.

'One night I saw her by my bedside and she stood there and looked kindly at me and apologized for the way she had treated me. I was in high school at the time, so I got up and went to school as usual. Later that morning, the principal called me to his office. I was to go home because my grandmother had died the night before.'

Jerdana had the apology from her grandmother that she was never able to give in life. Perhaps it helps our relatives to move on themselves. I feel sure it does.

In many hospitals, the body is left for several hours after death to enable the spirit to leave the body. I believe that sometimes the spirit chooses to 'hang around', taking a last look at everything or to say a last goodbye to relatives before moving higher into the spirit realms. I have several stories which fit into this category.

Lori emailed me her story.

My Little Privilege

'I felt very privileged to have been a mum, even if it was only for a short while. I recently lost my two-and-a-half-month-old son Michael Austin from SIDS [Sudden Infant Death Syndrome – sometimes known as "cot death"]. From the moment I laid eyes on him I knew he was special. He was a miracle baby. I had been praying for him for eighteen years. Then, to only have him for that length of time seemed so unfair, but now that I have my thoughts somewhat together, I just know he was sent here for a reason.

'That reason is still kind of blurry, but I'm slowly getting the picture. He was the sweetest little boy I'd ever seen. The night before his passing we sat on the couch, just the two of us, and with his head by my shoulder he would look up at me and pucker his lips wanting a kiss. I would say, "Oh, Michael," and smile and kiss him. He'd smile, stretch his neck and kiss me and we'd do it again and again for two hours.

'I miss him terribly, and would do anything to have him back. But I have found peace in knowing he is right here with me. He lets me know. He has quite the personality.

'Jacky, I would do it all over again, even knowing that I would lose him. I don't think I'm crazy thinking that God needed an angel here on earth, and let me have it for him. Some of us dream of angels. I was blessed enough to have held one.'

Wendy's father announced his death to her. He was able to see the light from the other side and his loved ones coming to collect him.

Seeing the Light

'I was with my dad when he died on 2 October 1997. As he had suffered a stroke he could not communicate. However, the day before he died I noticed him looking towards the corner of the ceiling in the hospital ward. I asked him what he could see, but he wasn't concentrating on me, his eyes appeared not to believe what he was looking at. Then he smiled in recognition and raised his hand as if to wave at someone. His eyes then turned to me and we held the eye contact. I was feeling bemused as I could not see anything in the corner of the room. Dad then said, "I am going now," quite clearly, although since his stroke two weeks previously he had not been able to speak. Later that night he went into a coma and died.'

Wendy's dad was able to see those coming to collect him and it is common for the dying to sit up or talk in the moments before passing, even if they were unable to do so before.

This next story relates to a child passing and, as we have seen before, their loss is particularly difficult to bear. Jackie's son was still a young boy when he died in hospital.

Warning from God

'It was around five in the evening. I was alone with Jerry in his hospital room ... my husband had gone to get something to eat. By this time, Jerry's illness had progressed to the point that he had painful ulcers in his mouth and could barely talk, but as I sat next to his bed, he spoke to me and said, just as clear as a bell, "Mama, I'm going to die."

'I said, "What?" and he repeated it ... "Mama, I'm going to die."

'Now, Jerry was too young to understand the meaning of what he had just told me, so where else could this have come from other than God? I didn't have time to say anything more because just then the doctor came into the room to examine Jerry and when he saw that he was having trouble breathing, he decided to admit him to ICU. Thirty-six hours later, Jerry was gone.

'I can't help but believe that I was being prepared for his death.'

Is it possible that our loved ones can have a premonition of their own passing? Did Sue's husband have a premonition of his death? Sometimes, when we look back, it appears as if a person has changed their normal routine for no apparent reason.

Packing the Suit

'My husband died suddenly in June 1994. He had been ill for about eighteen months prior to this and after finally getting to the root of his illness and being treated, he'd started to get better.

'To understand Bob a little better, let me explain. He was a kind, generous man who would do anything for anyone and give them his last pound if he could. A wonderful husband and loving father, but on the down side, when it came to work he was very committed and a workaholic. When it came to holidays and time off I had to organize things weeks in advance with him and sometimes beg and cajole for him to take time off.

'So consequently, it came as a great surprise when in June, after having returned to work in February following his illness, he rang me from work asking if we could go to Portsmouth to visit his parents so that they might see how much better he was. Expecting him to say he wanted to go in a few weeks' time, I was even more surprised when he said he wanted to go the following week. So I arranged for our two boys and the dog to stay with my parents and we left for Portsmouth on the Wednesday.

'When we packed he took his best suit, shirt, tie and shoes with us, although we were going nowhere where he would have needed to wear them. These hung on the back of the bedroom door from the time we got to his parents' house. For the few days we were there we visited friends and family and everyone said how well he looked and he told everyone how much better he was feeling.

'Then, on the Saturday evening whilst out with friends, he dropped dead with a heart attack and although the ambulance crew and hospital did everything they could he was declared dead at 22.10. The clothes that he brought with him were given to the undertakers for him to wear.

'Was there some subconscious need for him to do this? I believe so, as I feel he wanted to be with his family when he was cremated, so that he could be scattered with his grandmother at the same cemetery.

'A couple of nights after he died I woke up to see this very bright light in front of me with the shadow of what I can only describe as a church window behind it. Walking through this light was a very tall man with a beard. As he drew closer, Bob was laid at his feet and he bent down and opened his chest, drawing his heart into his hand. He then picked him up with his very large hands and folded Bob into his arms, walking back into the light with him. I knew then that he had not suffered and that wherever he was now, he was safe and happy. I know this was not a dream but a vision that was meant to bring me comfort.

'The next event occurred a few months later when I was

trying to make a decision as to whether I should buy the house I now live in (as it's near to my parents). I woke up to see Bob standing at the end of the bed looking at me and as I sat up he smiled as if to say it was okay, that moving was a good idea. As I spoke to him he backed away from the bed and I got up to follow and he backed out of the door. When I got to the door he had disappeared into the boys' bedroom and I knew then I would buy this house.

'Sometimes I see him in dreams but these dreams seem elusive and I'm not sure what they are about, but I know they are not ordinary dreams. Sometimes these dreams make me cry but I feel it's through happiness not sadness.'

These wonderful experiences give us great comfort when we need it most. Our loved ones don't want to interfere with our choices, just back up what we need to do. They seem to show that they support us in whatever way we choose to live our lives. Sometimes that guiding hand seems to say, 'Everything is going to be just fine.'

Gentle Touches

Adam felt a touch on his shoulder, like Steve, earlier in the chapter.

Supportive Hand

'My first encounter happened in 1982, on the day of my father's death. It was late in the afternoon and I was standing in the lounge on my own looking out the window. In the kitchen stood my mum and a friend of my dad's. I had my back to them when I felt a hand on my shoulder; I turned around expecting to see either of them standing next to me. They were still in the kitchen chatting and there was no way one of them could have touched me and gone back to the kitchen without me seeing them move. Also, what would have been the point?

'The feeling of that hand was very real to me and yet there was no one there. I still feel now as I did then that it was my dad trying to comfort me.'

Sometimes these early visitations can involve an actual vision of some sort. Donata's brother visited her in pure spirit but she still recognized him.

Brother in Golden Light

'When my brother died, he came to me the day after. I "saw" him as a golden ovoid shape. At the time I was awake and sitting in our living room with others, who didn't see him.

'He "spoke" to me in my head, but in his normal voice, and joked with me. He told me he was very happy, and as he said this the golden orb glowed. It only lasted about three minutes, but I've never had any doubt that it was my brother. I've never doubted the reality of life after death since then.'

Even though our loved ones have just passed they can also show themselves in the form of a physical appearance. Sheri saw her grandfather floating outside her window after he died. She told me, 'I had just gone to bed and was wide awake. It kind of scared me at first, but then I felt a sort of peace and calm afterwards as if he was telling us that he's still around and he's okay.'

She was more prepared when her father died and she saw him walk through the living room the night after he died. He also looked just as he did before death but much healthier.

Here's Emma's story.

Hand on My Shoulder

'A few months ago my partner and I had gone to bed after watching a film and he virtually fell asleep straight away. I was sat up in bed looking out the window thinking about my grandad who had died about eleven years ago. I started to cry gently as I usually do, and then I felt this hand grab my shoulder. I could feel the grip and the warmth from it and then I heard a voice say, "Sshhhhhhhh." I spun round to see if it was my partner but he was asleep, snoring, so I knew it wasn't him and there was no one else in the room with us. I realized it was my grandad telling me to stop crying and that everything is okay.'

Spirits like to make a lot of noise when they can – although this can be more frightening, even if it seems to give a better validation. When the noise is heard by more than one person it is easier to cope with.

Lyn was scared when she heard the spirit of her mother moving around in the kitchen.

Cleaning in the Kitchen

'When my mother passed on, the morning after her funeral my husband Ken awoke to hear her doing her usual things in our kitchen ... I freaked out! Wild horses wouldn't have dragged me out into that kitchen, as I didn't want to see a ghost, even though I loved my mother dearly. So I pushed Ken out of bed and he went to see Mum's ghost in the kitchen. As he arrived the sounds stopped and there was nothing to see! He called me out to the kitchen to have a look and sure enough, there was no spiritual mother.

'I look back on this incident and laugh and think how silly I was back in those days. I have seen many "ghosts" since then and heaps of them were total strangers ... and yet at that time I was scared of seeing my own beloved mother.

'Now I know they are merely people in their spirit form and they hold no fear for me any more. We learn and we grow in spiritual knowledge. My mother has since returned and that was pure joy, never fear; a blessing.'

These next two people crossed over very closely together

and an interesting phenomenon developed as a result. Here is Kirsty's story.

Two's Company

'On 10 April, my uncle died. At the same time, his father was also very ill in hospital, although we hadn't told him about it as he was so ill himself.

'On the Sunday night we were in the hospital with my grandad. The doctors had given us a family room as we knew grandad was dying, so we just wanted to be there for him, having already lost my uncle. I was totally washed out with grief and was trying to get a bit of sleep.

'We had been taking it in turns to stay with grandad and I must have dropped off. I suddenly woke up, although I have no idea why, and on the cupboard was the word BOO in large colourful letters! I hadn't noticed it before, and I glanced at the clock, which read 11.15 pm.

'I drifted back to sleep until 3 am, and when I woke up the writing had disappeared. I assumed I must have dreamt it, until I told my other uncle about it later on in the day. He was amazed and told me, 'We used to call your uncle that name a long time ago!'

'The next day we lost my grandad but in his last breath he said, "Boo," so even though we never told him his son had died we think he knew.'

As in the other cases, I imagine that Kirsty's uncle had waited around to collect his relative.

Carol's friend came to warn her he had died by playing out a dream scene for her, but it wasn't too long before he came back to let her know he was doing okay.

Don't Worry

'A good friend of mine, Roy, had been suffering from a brain tumour for a few months. For no apparent reason, one Saturday night I had a dream that I was looking at his medical notes, and someone said I would be in trouble for doing so. Then a doctor appeared and said not to worry as Roy had died.

'I then saw Roy who looked very old and tired. The very next day it was announced he had in fact died on Sunday morning.

'After around six months I had another dream where Roy was sitting on a riverbank smiling and looking like his old self. He told me not to worry as dying was not painful, and he looked so happy.'

We soon look like our old selves once we pass over to the heavenly realms. A short session of healing and we appear as good as new!

CHAPTER 9

Children and the ADC

Children seldom misquote. In fact, they usually repeat word for word what you shouldn't have said.

Author unknown

More and more children are being born with enhanced psychic ability. Younger children, particularly before they start school, are able see, hear and feel things that others don't, or can't. Some people say that children have so recently left their spiritual homes to live in the physical body, that this is why it is easier for them to 'tune in'. Of course, children have no reason to lie about their experiences. They say it how it is.

I run an internet group for parents of children with enhanced psychic abilities, so that they can discuss their children's special skills and offer coping strategies for each other. Sometimes it is very confusing for the parent of a child who picks up psychic phenomena, especially if the parent doesn't have any experience in this area.

The afterlife communication experience is just as

common with children as it is with adults. Here are some special experiences.

Chatting with the Afterlife

Cierra was only three months old when her mother noticed she was different to her two older children. The young baby seemed distracted constantly by something unseen – laughing at the empty space to her side. It was only after photographs showed a strange mist in the space that occupied Cierra's attention, that her mother Melody suspected that something else was going on!

Taking her cue from Cierra's baby conversations, Melody built up an impressive collection of 'spirit photographs' showing impressions of a swirling white and green energy alongside Cierra (some of these are on my website: www.jackynewcomb.co.uk). Cierra says that these swirling mists are 'Jane', a spirit friend who is always around her.

Melody told me, 'When I first started noticing her reacting to an unseen presence, she would smile and coo and reach out and seemed to follow something with her eyes. This would happen when she was in her crib. I'd think she was asleep but she was awake and interacting with whoever it was.

'She also did this in her baby swing and in her bouncy chair and sometimes while sitting on my lap or my husband's. She would lean towards the presence and we could actually feel like there was someone standing before us.'

As Cierra got a little older, it became more apparent that

the spirit visitors were real people. Melody and her family began to recognize some of the visitors that Cierra was communicating with.

'When she was nine months old she was sitting in her bouncy chair and she looked into our dining room. This is the time she laughed out loud and said, "I see you, Grandpa – you funny!"'

Yet Cierra had never met her grandfather as he died in 1998, before Cierra was born. Most of the other spirit visitors are also strangers to the toddler – strangers in the body, but not in spirit it seems.

'It was after this encounter that she started having an affinity for things with clowns on them. She deliberately grabbed a clown doll in a store and when we held up different 'drinky' holders for her to choose from she picked the one with the clown on it. We took her cue and bought her bottles and other things with clowns on them. When my father was alive, he often dressed up as a clown at charity parties for children.'

Melody told me, 'She has clearly distinguished between my mother ("Grandma") and Levi's mother, whom she did meet ("Gramma"). My mom loved the colour purple and whenever she is around Cierra refers to her as Grandma in the purple dress. She also never met my grandfather who we called Paw-Paw, or my grandmother who we called MiMi. She has spoken to both of them by our pet names even though we really never mentioned them to her. She calls my grandpa "Paw-Paw O" (his first name was Osie) and my grandma she calls Mi-Mi-Mary (her first name was Mary).'

It's not just family who have benefited from the messages passed by spirit to this two-year-old toddler. Melody says, 'She has given messages to people who were just over visiting. One was to this guy who smoked like a chimney. She came up to him one night and said, "You know, Joyce wanted you to quit smoking; you really should," in a chiding voice. He turned white and he quit smoking a couple days later and has not started up again. It turns out Joyce was his mother and she had always hounded him about quitting smoking because it made her sick and eventually caused her death.'

Harsh words? Maybe, but would this gentleman's mother have said the same words to him if she were still alive? Probably, and that's what makes the messages real!

Throughout this, Melody still manages to keep a sense of humour, and I had a bit of a laugh when I read her latest email. She told me, 'We did have one recent sighting of "Jane". My hubby and I had turned out the lights and sat by the fire to watch television and we both saw a little blonde girl come into the living room, put her hands on the baby's playpen and smile. It kind of freaked me out to actually SEE her as I haven't seen her before. She turned and walked into the closet door. I also believe the closet is where many of the spirits come and go from. It is our coat closet, and it is filled with all the other junk that we don't have room for around our cosy little house, so it must be crowded in there for them!'

I asked Melody to tell Cierra about me, and let her know that I was going to be writing about her and to check it was okay. Even though she is such a small child, I felt she deserved the respect that I give all adults who contribute to the book. I received this interesting reply.

'She knows about you. I first told her about you when we started talking through emails. I told her that you were going to write about what she has seen and try to help people be happy. She says that you are "over the water" but you are going to fly over here and be where we are for a while. She also says to make sure you tell people about love: it's important that love is still there when people go over to the sparkly place. I think she is trying to say that love doesn't die with your loved ones, they don't forget you, they still love you, even after death.'

I was pleased with my message from the toddler. The 'sparkly place' is what she calls heaven – she seems to have a wise understanding of the realms of spirit, and the concept of love for one so young! Oh, and yes, we live in different countries – I am 'over the water', but would very much like to visit and write more about Cierra and her insight at some future date, but it seems that she knows about this already! In the meantime, her spiritual guides are keeping her up-to-date with my future plans!

There is a story I featured in my book *An Angel Treasury*. I remember my daughter was only two when my own grandmother died. It was not a sad funeral, my Nan was in her nineties when she passed, and she told us she was ready to leave for the spirit planes. She died peacefully in bed at home. We celebrated her earthly life and toasted her new heavenly life where she would be with the spirit family she so badly wanted to be reunited with.

After the funeral, my young daughter and I were playing on the floor in the living room when she suddenly pointed to the ceiling in surprise.

'Look Mummy, a "fairy-man!"' came the startled voice of my toddler.

Had she seen an angel or my grandmother in her spirit self? I firmly believed she had. My daughter hadn't been to the funeral, nor did she have any understanding of what a 'spirit' might be. She just explained to me what she could see in the only language she had. That's what makes children's experiences so brilliant!

When my daughters were babies I would be feeding them late into the night and both of them would often stop and turn their heads away from me and laugh as if someone were amusing them in the dark! Of course now I realize that this was probably not my imagination.

Melissa's contact came right out of the blue.

The Man with the Pipe

'I had a newborn baby and I was sleeping in the nursery with him when my three-year-old boy came and crawled into bed with me. Looking across the hall and into our dining room, he asked me, "Mommy, who's that man?" I didn't see anyone but my son persisted. "That man who lives here, he said he loves to tickle our baby!" I didn't want to scare my son and so I changed the subject.

'A few weeks later, the daughter of the man who used to live here came to visit. As she passed the dining room, she stopped and looked in the very same place and said, "Daddy always loved to sit at the end of that table and read his paper and smoke his pipe – I can still see my daddy sitting at the end of this table, even today. He loved to sit on the sun porch and watch TV all spring and summer on his little black and white TV."'

Melissa thought this was a bit of a coincidence and decided to question her son further.

'After she left, I called my little boy into the room and asked him to show me where the man sat. He pointed to the end of the table, and told me, "He wears pants like Daddy wears to church, a jacket the colour of grass, a hat like Grandma wears in the garden, but I don't know what's wrong with his mouth ... what's that smoking stick in his mouth, mama?"

'I was amazed and decided to follow up the story further, and see if I could track down a photograph. I discovered that he always wore the same outfit: khaki pants, a green shirt, a straw hat; and smoked a pipe everywhere he went!'

Like I said earlier, children say what they see using the language that is available to them. These things are too random to be made up, and seem too much of a coincidence.

Maria told me about her little one.

Blowing Kisses

'My daughter of twenty months keeps on talking to someone and blowing kisses. She seems to bend over, as if to cuddle someone.'

Maria wondered if it was her mother who never got to see her little grandchild in life. Although Maria's mother knew about the baby, she passed when she was just three weeks pregnant.

'Just recently I've become more aware of it as my daughter is at the age of nearly talking. When I put her down at night I switch on the intercom and some times I can hear whispers in the room, followed by my daughter whispering back. My daughter does not normally whisper, as she is very loud, but when I go to check on her she is lying there awake pointing to the corner of the room!'

Children's Pets

Many children have 'invisible pets' as well as 'invisible friends'. Are some of these invisible friends spirits, rather than the make believe people and animals which most adults consider them to be? Beverly thinks so.

Jessie

Beverly was perplexed when her two-year-old son suddenly developed a 'spirit dog' for a friend.

'He insists on taking an empty dog lead out with us when we take our real dog for a walk. He says she's called Jessie. He also shouts names that don't mean anything to us, like Margaret and John. He sometimes says, "Who's that talking?" when I can't hear anyone! On one occasion, he told me that "John" was shouting "Jim" or "Jimmy".'

You'll find more pet stories later, especially in the next chapter, Animals and the ADC.

Relatives Saying Goodbye to Children

Stacy felt that she was visited by her grandma and her grandpa. Sometimes our loved ones come to say goodbye, especially if we didn't get to say goodbye in life. I feel sure that they are aware of our distress. Dream visitations are an easy and comfortable way for us to receive their communication.

Tobacco

'Ten years ago my grandmother passed away. She was only sixty-seven and had cancer for six years. I was very sad because I never got to say goodbye to her.

'We got a phone call from the hospital, who told us that she had been taken in. They said the cancer had spread so we decided to go to the hospital right away. My grandmother lived thirteen hours away and as we were preparing to leave we had another call. She had passed away already.

'I never went to the funeral where they spread her ashes on the flowers she loved. I just blocked everything out for many years. Not long after, my grandpa also passed away from cancer because he smoked and, my guess is, because he missed my grandmother.

'About six years ago I was alone with my cat when I became aware of the smell of antiseptic and tobacco smoke. My grandpa always smelt of this when he came to visit so I thought of him right away. It was a clear smell and I hadn't smelt it since he died.

'Then, about six months ago, I dreamt that my grandpa and grandma were sitting there, saying goodbye to me. All I could see was black behind them and it was clear who they were and what they were wearing. This was the first time I had dreamt of them.

'Then last night I dreamt of my grandma only. I dreamt I was living with my parents still and my grandma was standing outside by my truck. She was wearing a tight, flowered shirt with brown pants. I asked her where she was going and she said she had to go. I asked, "Please could you stay so we could talk for a bit, and I could ask many questions?" Then I woke up.'

Janet wrote and told me about her son's girlfriend's daughter, Hollie. Hollie is very aware of a special protector in her life. Janet told me, 'She keeps saying there is a lady at the top of their stairs, and this lady gives her pennies!' Oh, and Hollie is just two years old.

Sometimes our children can bring us warnings. With the innocence of a child, everything seems so simple.

Going to See Grandpa

'As an infant my son would lay on my grandma's bed (in the room she and her late husband shared) and would giggle and coo up above him ... I always believed he was playing with my grandfather.

'Then, in March of last year my son, aged four, came up to me out of the blue. I was sitting at the computer and he had been playing. He said, "Mom ... great grandma is old."

'I agreed, "Yes she is."

'Then he said, "Mom ... great grandma is going to die."

'I was sort of taken aback. My grandmother was very healthy and was having no problems, and my son had also only seen her a handful of times.

'I said to him, "That's not very nice."

'But he turned and looked at me dead between the eyes and calmly said, "It's okay mommy, she's going to go to heaven."

'We don't go to a church of any kind and I found this humorous. Since my grandma was lively and could take a good joke I called her the next day to tell her what Mitchell had said. We joked a little about it. The day after talking to her (two days after he told me) my grandmother had a stroke and died.

'My son was fine about the whole thing and, when I told him about why I was upset and crying, my four year old

> proceeded to calm me and tell me it was okay because she was going to heaven to see my dad (he meant my grandpa).'

Children can be amazingly astute, can't they? More children's psychic experiences later.

CHAPTER 10

Animals and the ADC

Animals are reliable, many full of love, true in their affections, predictable in their actions, grateful and loyal. Difficult standards for people to live up to ...

Alfred A Montapert

I miss my cats. They both disappeared on the same day and I never saw them again, but I did feel one of them. Several years after they went missing, I was surprised when I felt one of the cats jump up onto the bed and wake me up. He circled round and sat down. I could hear him purring and padding at the covers. I sat up and reached over to give him a stroke before I realized I could see nothing on the bed. The spirit of my dead cat had just popped back to say goodbye and I was very happy about it.

After our beloved pets pass on, they go to the heavenly realms in the same way that our human friends do, and in that same way, they can come back to visit, to reassure us that they are okay. As with all of the stories in this book, the accounts are real. Here are some pet visitation stories.

Kathy's cat stayed around for a while after death, too.

Shadow Cat

'When our cat Pepper died, she came back for several visits. My daughter was the first to see her. She appeared as a dark shadow crossing a doorway or going around a corner. My husband and I were the next to see her. She came frequently, but as time went on her visits dwindled. I think it helped my daughter deal with her death.'

Antonia's special childhood friend visited her in dreams. Like humans, they can choose how they wish to appear to us.

Young Again Dog

'Robby, the dog I grew up with, was a very friendly companion. He was my best friend, my only friend for many years. I was really upset when he died. He is the only one of our pets that comes back to visit. He always comes in the same dream; running around the horse chestnut tree beside the paddock at my dad's house, where I grew up.

'This is a happy memory of being playful and childlike. Inside, that house was full of sadness, so I think that is why Robby comes to play outside by the tree, running through the leaves in the sunshine. And he comes back so fit and healthy with a glossy coat, not as the old man he was when he passed over.'

Linda's dog also visited her in dreams.

Still Bringing Comfort

'We lost our little Westie Sammy when he was just over thirteen years old and he came to me in dreams a few times when he passed over. It's been a difficult time with my mum in hospital, and I am worrying about my father who has senile dementia.

'I miss my little dog as I would tell him my troubles. He would just give his love without question. One day I said to his photo, "I wish I could see him." Then a few days later I had yet another dream where he was on the stairs. I picked him up and kissed him on the top of his head like I would do if he was here. When I put him down he ran back upstairs.

'He gave me a lovely blessing by coming to see me. We are still connected, and I can tell that he must have loved me, to make this journey again to see me, and I can still tell him my troubles.'

Susie was a much-loved dog belonging to my mum and dad. She was a funny-looking thing with a curly, unattractive tail, but she was lovely and gentle and a family member for a long time. We were used to being greeted at the door. She would bark and rush up with her tail wagging. Several weeks after she died it was hard to remember she was no longer with us. Many of the family would still feel her around as we walked in the front door – she would rub round our legs and we could feel her bang her wagging tail against us! My mother even saw her once. Susie wasn't in any hurry to leave the family home, which was fine with us.

Years later I had my own dog, and after my own little dog 'Lady' died I wrote this email to a friend.

Uncle's Photo a Sign

'I had my first sign today that my little dog has arrived safely on the other side. I asked my dad's brother (my uncle Eric who has passed) if he would let me know that she had arrived safely. This afternoon a magazine telephoned and asked me for a photo of my uncle to include in an article about afterlife communication that I had written (six months ago). This was a strange coincidence after I had asked him about my dog just today.

'The photo was poor quality and she asked if I had any others (I wasn't sure). I walked over to my photo albums on a shelf (eight of them, all the same) and picked one at random. I then opened the album, also at random – and there was another picture of uncle Eric! (It was the only other photograph I had of him, as far as I know.) He has been passed over for many years now so it did strike me as a bit of a coincidence that I was asked about him today, especially as I had asked for a sign! But of course we know it isn't coincidence. No doubt I will get more signs over the next few days so I will let you know.'

Of course, as you have guessed, I did get more signs. Next my little dog appeared to me in a vision whilst I was drifting off to sleep.

Been Here Before

I was drifting off to sleep, about three weeks after Lady had died. I still felt guilty at having her put down but in my heart I knew it was the right thing to do as she was having many problems. I'd thought about her every day and every time I thought about her I cried. I remembered how I'd held her at the vets as they gave her that final lethal injection. Afterwards, I curled her up in a sleeping position on the table so she looked like she had fallen asleep.

But then, as I lay in my own bed she appeared in front of me. It wasn't a dream and I was wide awake. Behind Lady were loads of other family dogs and they seemed to be almost queuing up behind her. If dogs could wave and smile I would say this was what they were doing. I know it sounds crazy, silly even, but this is how I felt.

I noticed immediately that another childhood dog, Candy, who had bitten me as a child, was missing from this crowd. It was then that I 'felt' an explanation. I was told that my dear dog 'Lady' had been my dog previously and that she had actually been our dog Candy. It was as if they were telling me that Lady had been reincarnated from the soul of Candy.

They went on to explain that as Candy had bitten me and my two sisters (we all had stitches in our faces), as well as other people, she had to come back and make it up to me in some way.

We chose Lady from a rescue centre after we had been burgled. It was strange because I rang round all the centres with a 'shopping list' of the sort of dog I wanted. Small, like a cat, female, very gentle and sweet and short haired, so she didn't leave a lot of hair. After several weeks, one of the rescue centres called to tell us that they had the perfect dog. That dog was Lady and it was strange because we didn't even look at other dogs, just the one.

Lady always walked with a sort of limp. The rescue centre felt that she had been treated badly before we homed her. When Lady came to me in this vision, it was explained to me that she had chosen her life so that she might learn humility.

Of course I had read a lot about reincarnation but it hadn't occurred to me until that time that our pets might follow a similar path of karma that we had ourselves!

The visit was to say goodbye but also to ask if she had been finally forgiven for biting me as a child! I couldn't believe it but of course I forgave her.

That wasn't the end of the story. Several weeks later I was working on an article about spirit artists; psychic artists who drew pictures of passed-over loved ones and spiritual guides. Whilst I was interviewing the psychic artist Debbie Dean, she told me that she had a little black dog running around at her feet. 'I think this dog is for you!' she said.

I hadn't mentioned the death of my little dog a few weeks earlier so I asked if she could draw the dog and email me the image. I was completely stunned when I saw the picture. It was the perfect likeness of Lady. Lady had found another way to let me know she was okay. I was thrilled.

If you want to see Debbie's drawing next to photographs of my dog then you will find them at my website: www.jackynewcomb.co.uk.

Jill wrote to tell me about her friend's pet.

Home Again

'My friend Steff is a medium. She told me she lost her cat back in April. Later she had a dream in which her cat came to her. The cat indicated that she would come to her again and would have a black tail sticking straight up so she would recognize her. At the time, Steff didn't even want another cat.

'Last week, Steff finally felt strong enough to go to the animal shelter to find another cat. She was led to a cage containing a white cat that had a black marking on its back. As Steff approached the cage, the cat's tail went straight up and it was BLACK! She was stunned and immediately adopted this cat.'

Our animals are very psychic too. They seem to have the ability to see and hear outside of our own range of senses. Dogs particularly are known for their acute hearing. I always think of those 'silent' dog whistles – silent to us that is, but not for the dog. Many dogs and cats will acknowledge unseen visitors, too. Cats will show their displeasure by hissing and lifting the hair on their backs to spirit visitors unseen by the human eye. Dogs will bark or wag their tails in happiness, or growl. Isn't it strange when they stare at the blank wall behind you?

My friend Wendy is pretty open minded and quite happy to see the spirit of a black dog run from the back door of her new bungalow right through to the front of the house.

'It's okay,' she reassures everyone. 'It belongs to the previous owner!' I guess it didn't realize that its mistress had moved house.

This dog certainly got the message that its owner had passed over. Debbie's father was home alone when her mother died – alone except for the dog.

Announcing

'Two of my sisters went to tell him Mom had died. He was sitting at the kitchen table dressed in his overalls, waiting for them – he knew already that my mother had died because he said her dog had started howling. I don't know if the dog howled because it knew what had happened, but when the dog howled dad certainly knew mom had died.'

Sensitive Owners

Nick's family dog Jessie had been a part of the family for thirteen years when she died. Jessie was a black Labrador cross, and very gentle and loving. Her owners felt guilty as many of us do when we have to have our pets euthanized. Nick told me:

Waiting for the Right Moment

'We always felt she was "stuck" somehow when she died, almost as if she hadn't realized she was dead. She'd died but hadn't gone anywhere.

'It doesn't surprise me that she was stuck. Both my wife Dilly and I felt that we had betrayed her in some way because we'd had her put down. It was a very difficult decision to make and even though she was obviously dying we found it hard to end her life, but by now she was obviously suffering. When the vet put her down, Jessie cried even though the vet said that they never do that normally. Maybe our guilt kept her here.

'About three or four weeks after she died I had just asked my spirit guides, before we went to sleep, if there was anything we could do for her. That night I had a dream, and in the dream she was just on a settee as if she was waiting for me. I felt that she knew what was going on ... it was as if she was waiting for something to happen. I cuddled her and I felt her.

'You know in a dream you don't feel things but this was different. I could feel her wet nose on my face and I told her that she was dead and had to move on. It was as if she understood it was time to go, and when I woke up there was a different atmosphere in the house, as if she had finally gone to wherever she was supposed to go, and I did feel much happier after it happened.'

With Love ...

Lynette is psychic and has always felt that she communicated with animals on a spiritual level. Her home is full of animal spirits still.

Our Animal Spirit Visitors

'Our home is readily available to visits from spirit animals; visitors to our home also see them. This has become so much the case that I give a friendly warning to folk who stay with us overnight that they shouldn't be alarmed if they feel an invisible or ghostly animal jump on the bed during the night and even walk up and over them, because this was what our animals did when on earth and they still do it. I don't want our visitors scared out of their wits by the sudden actions of our spirit animals!

'The latest incident happened in the school holidays just past. Our eleven-year-old grandson happened to mention that he hears a dog that barks at the back of our place, and my husband said, "Oh, you mean the one that sounds like Ben when he barks." (Ben is our deceased dog/cross Alpine Dingo, a very gentle animal.) Our grandson replied, "Yes, and by the way, I've seen Ben since I've been here, but I only saw his fluffy white tail going down the hall. I've seen him here before, but all I ever see is his fluffy white tail, nothing else."

'This is how it happens sometimes. Part of the animal is seen, or a watery image of the whole animal is seen, as happened with our toddler granddaughter. Our daughter saw her chasing the spirit of our cat Samantha down our hall before we moved to our present home, as she had done when our beloved tortoiseshell and white cat had been alive. This happened not long after our cat had passed on.

'Our eldest grandson was only young when Ben crossed over and he knew nothing about the movements of spirit animals or that they could exist. I was in the kitchen and he came out to me with a puzzled expression on his face and said, "Nanny, I just saw Ben go into the bathroom!" Now, our bathroom door was always kept shut when our grandson was there, because he had had a nasty fall one day there on the tiles, so this meant that he had seen Ben's spirit pass through the door. This was what had puzzled him, rather than the fact that he knew that Ben was dead.

'Samantha was never allowed to sit on the pillow on our bed, but the night after she died I felt her jump up beside my face on my pillow, and immediately I could smell the strong odour that she had when she was dying!

'I said, "Samantha, you get off there, you know you aren't allowed to sit on my pillow." I felt her jump off immediately, although of course I then felt so sad, because despite the sudden overpowering aroma, I wanted her to share my pillow ... it was merely what I would have said if she was alive.

'On another occasion, my husband saw Ben "superimposed"

over Samantha on our bed, and we often feel spirit animals announce their presence to us by rubbing firmly up against our legs or jumping on our bed when we are in it.

'One morning I was about to step out into our hallway and found it packed with Ben, another dog, and several cats! Some cats were sitting; another was rubbing back and forth up against Ben's chest, as he and the other dog sat "Sphinx-like" there. I couldn't walk past without passing through the lot of them, so I waited until they disappeared before coming out into the hall.

'I never charge for my psychic assistance, but at one time a friend asked me to request "Healing from the Beyond" for a very ill Alsatian dog, which I did. I then left it in hands beyond my own.

'I was in our shower and not thinking of this dog at all, when suddenly I saw this lovely Alsatian, standing there and wagging his tail with a happy doggie grin on his face and I thought, "I wonder how he is?" I contacted my friend via email and she told me that this lovely dog had passed on at the time I saw him in my shower – the dog was in the USA and I live in Australia. Distance is nothing to spirit; I have had many long-distance experiences with them. Many times I have been taken to where I was needed without my requesting it and this always surprises me. I never take Spirit for granted and am always grateful for my Gift.

'I asked for protection one evening and a Bengal tiger appeared before me in our bedroom. I then rolled over and went contentedly to sleep; I knew my Spirit Guide had provided the protection I needed. I was sent a lion friend on other occasions.

'Animal communication is a wonderful privilege although I believe it must be earned by our love and care of those who have souls the same as we do. They merely look different and speak a different language.'

...and Protection

Jill also saw a big cat and she too felt the animal had been sent as a special protection for her family. Here is her experience.

Big Cat Protection

'One day, I was meditating as I try to do every afternoon at about 2 pm. I rarely see anything like many of my psychic friends, but sometimes a face will come into focus and it is quite amazing. I never know who it is, but I am tickled just to see something. This particular day, the face of a cougar came into focus and I was quite awed by him. I had no idea why I was seeing a cougar.

'A week later, early in the morning, I stumbled out of bed and walked down the darkened hall to see if my daughter was awake. I do this every morning. The light was on in the kitchen, casting enough light for me to see. I could see light under her bedroom door.

'As I approached the door, my eyes were drawn to something sitting by her door. I peered down and it looked like a house cat! We don't have a cat, and I immediately thought a neighbour's cat had somehow gotten into our house and it startled me. Suddenly, the cat was BIG. It was sitting on its haunches with its back to me. Slowly, it turned its head and glowing blue eyes stared at me from the exact same cougar face I had seen in my meditation! This all happened quite quickly and I was immediately frightened this cougar was going to attack me.

'I ran to the living room and jumped up on the couch ... like that would save me from a charging cougar! I screamed out to Lindsay ... which seems so silly now! She did not hear me, thank goodness. I was shaking so hard until I got a hold of myself. I thought, "Now, Jill, you know that wasn't a real cougar ... it was a spirit cougar ... so calm down!"

'This happened right at the beginning of Lindsay's freshman year of high school. She had been worried about high school, and I theorize the cougar came to assure me Lindsay was always protected.'

Patricia is very sensitive to the energy of animals too.

Cats and Hedgehogs

'My first experience was with my dear cat Spike, who had a liver tumour and had to be put to sleep. For a couple of days afterwards my cousin and I would catch a glimpse of him out of the corner of our eyes, sitting in his usual spots. He looked healthy and happy and eventually stopped coming by.

'Then my cousin has a hedgehog, Duncan (yes, a hedgehog!) that we will occasionally hear snuffling under the couch like he used to do – it sounds like a sizzle in a frying pan and is unmistakable.'

Animal Messengers

Another friend told me a story about her brother-in-law. I believe that our own loved ones will work with animal spirit to make their communication with us.

The 'Goodbye' Owls

'When Joseph was a young boy, he received a book titled, *I Heard the Owl Call my Name*. He loved the simple story of a priest who worked with an Indian tribe in northern Canada. It was tribal belief that if you heard an owl call your name, you would die soon. One day, after years of serving the Indians, the priest walked through a forest into town and heard an owl calling his name. He died soon after from a sudden illness.

'The story captivated Joseph and he shared the book with his father, also named Joseph. His father loved the book too and they both read it many times over the years and discussed it.

'The day after Christmas in 1988, Joseph's father died suddenly of a heart attack. Shocked, Joseph paced the living room at his parent's home. Finally, he slipped onto the back porch and looked up to the heavens. There, silhouetted in the moonlight were two lovely owls. Joseph immediately recognized these wise birds as his father and grandfather. "I just knew they had come to bid me farewell," Joseph said. "They did it in a way that I would recognize." Joseph called his wife and sister onto the porch, and they too had this same feeling.

'Soon, one of the owls visited Joseph's other sister and sat on her porch rail staring into her living room. An owl had never landed there before. She was drawn to the window and knew it was her father.

'For three years, on the anniversary of his father's death, Joe would hear an owl outside his back door and knew it was his father. On the fourth year, he walked onto his deck and suddenly a bird flew within a foot of him and landed on a tree branch ten feet away. It was a small owl. The bird stared and nodded, and Joseph knew. "It was Dad's final farewell. I never saw the owls after that. But it was a comfort to know my dad was okay, and was still looking out for me." '

Katrina had her own bird visitor … and a butterfly.

Is it You, Dad?

'I have a dove that is about ten to twenty feet away from me every day. This happens if I am at home or at my mum's house which is about five miles away. My father passed recently and I wondered if this could be him watching over me.

'Then a strange butterfly landed on my leg as I was walking to the mailbox. It was a yellow swallowtail, and it just landed on my thigh (while I was walking) and it regarded me with its "little butterfly face" as I stood there still, not wanting to disturb it. I had time to call for my cousin to see this crazy butterfly before it flapped at me a couple of times and fluttered off.'

Here is an unusual sign, this time using a fly! Lynn dropped me an email to tell me all about it.

Fly Paper

'I just wanted to let you know of an experience I had the other night. I lost my dear mum only last month, Jacky, and have just discovered spiritual church and mediums, so this is all new to me.

'Mum and I were so close, and one of the things she always used to say to me was, "Don't worry, you worry too much and you'll make yourself ill." This was picked up on at the very first meeting I had with a medium, so I knew that it was mum. Anyway, back to the experience. I was lying in bed reading your book, *An Angel Saved My Life*, and was on page 200. I must just add that I wasn't feeling too happy as my husband and I had had words earlier that day. All of a sudden a tiny little fly landed on the page. I watched it climb onto my thumb, then it jumped down and walked down the page a bit then stopped still for what seemed like ages.

'The words on the page where the little fly had rested said, "not to worry", the fifteenth line down the page. Then, as quick as it arrived, it flew away. My heart lifted and I said, "Thanks mum." I would love to think this was a message from her.

'On another occasion I felt something brush over my hand whilst I was in bed thinking of her and I've seen a couple of lights; one was sort of floaty but small, the other one was like a star looks to us outside but this was in the bedroom and was gone in a second.'

When I first read this I wondered, 'Could a fly send a message from the "other side"?' But then I thought, 'Why not?'

I hear quite a lot of butterfly stories. Here's a story about a moth, sent to me by Kim.

Moth Coincidence

'My father passed away almost one month ago. On the eve of his funeral my brother had a dream that a moth entered his coffin in the chapel of rest, the undertakers could not get it out so they left it.

'This next part of the story is real and not the dream.

'After the funeral all the family went to my mother's home to comfort her. When my brother-in-law entered the house a moth was stuck on his shoe it flew up to his face then over to a plant in the lounge and fluttered round the room. As it wasn't the time of year for moths we do wonder if it was a visitation from my father. I've also had a dream about a butterfly, and a few strange coincidences concerning butterflies keep happening.'

Butterfly experiences are common after the loss of a loved

one and I have several stories in my files. Here is another one, this time sent by Moira – strangely, another person who was prompted to write after reading my last book.

Butterflies and Birds

'I have been reading your book *An Angel Saved My Life* and in it you say that the people whom we have loved and lost often show themselves as a bird or possibly butterflies.

'Well, I just have to say I have never seen a robin in my life and I was sat in my car one Sunday when I noticed something move on the ground. When I looked down it was a robin! It sat there for what seemed a long time, just looking at me, and then hopped underneath my car.

'I didn't think anything of it at the time until I read what you had said in your book. I was stunned, and stunned even more when I was sitting at work gazing out of the front door when there was another robin on the fence outside, just looking at me. Since then it has visited me in the same spot on the fence twice. My partner's sister was also taken aback when I told her about this robin – she said one comes and sits on the fence just at the back of her kitchen window and looks at her for ages.

'My partner and his sister lost their dad twelve weeks before my dad passed away last year. I also lost a very dear friend about ten years ago. At her funeral she was in her coffin in front of the altar when a shaft of light came in through a window onto her coffin and a vivid blue butterfly flapped about in this shaft of light. I just knew it was my friend.'

Of course, robins are friendly birds and this could be a coincidence, but many of the stories involving birds and butterflies happen at a time when we have asked for a sign, or even at a time when we need comfort and reassurance. With each story of course we have to make up our own mind.

This chapter covers a wide range of experiences both with pets and other animals. Some are visits from the other side and sometimes the animal seems to be 'borrowed' by our own loving friends and relations to pass on their messages of comfort from the other side. Sometimes the message is just one of protection. Whatever the story, I know that this is just the beginning of a bigger exploration.

CHAPTER 11

Assorted ADCs

...While you do not know life,
how can you know about death?
Confucius

Our spiritual friends are very inventive when it comes to catching our attention. Many of these stories came with the words, 'You won't believe it, but...' or 'I can't prove it, but...'

We explored some of the fascinating stories in the chapter on Spiritual Electricians but that was just the tip of the iceberg, as they say. Our friends have so many more tricks up their sleeves and I love their inventiveness.

Of all the hundreds of stories that I have written about, I have never forgotten this one. It was sent to me several years ago now, and has been waiting in my files for the perfect moment to include it in a book. This is that perfect moment. Of course, Colin gave me permission to print his story but when I tried to contact the family again I could not trace them and they had changed email addresses which was really sad.

This is Colin's story about his son.

In Memory of Logan

'On 30 November 2002, my son, Logan, died in a motorcycle accident. He has sent many signs to say he has arrived safely on the other side.

'Logan and I are both well built. He was six feet eight inches and wore size sixteen shoes; I am not quite so big. Logan and I both loved kart racing, and because of our size, we were quite used to coming last or second to last when we raced. Two weeks before he died, we had a major kart race meeting at our track. We managed to get TV coverage from our local channel. I had to work that weekend but I entered Logan in the Heavy Class which we normally race in. You need six people to make a field and there were only two entries, so he had to either change to a Light Class (and never have a chance of winning) or try and get a different engine and race in a different class. I rang a fellow racer who had the different engines and he agreed to lend Logan one. We were so lucky, Logan blitzed the field and won a fantastic trophy. He was also the star of the show on the TV programme, even being interviewed three times during the filming.

'When he died, the TV channel "7 Taranaki" were marvellous. They came around on the Monday afternoon with a preview tape of the show which was scheduled to screen the week after his funeral. We were very apprehensive when we put it on, expecting to burst into tears. To our surprise we and other friends who had gathered to watch it were cheering him on and the joy on his face was overwhelming. Kismet is the word for this, because the meeting was supposed to be held in Palmerston North (NZ) but for some unknown reason, they had asked if we could do it. Palmerston North doesn't have a local TV channel so to get this on film was fantastic. One of Logan's goals in life was to win a trophy in karting, and he made it!

'The first sign he gave me when he passed over was his chest moving when he was lying in state at our home the night before his funeral. I was alone and talking to him. It was almost as if he was letting out a big sigh because of my grief.

'The funeral was amazing, we had great difficulty choosing music and eventually settled on "Tears from Heaven" by Eric Clapton; "You'll Never Walk Alone" by Daniel O'Donnell, and my choice was "My Buddy" by Dr John.

'There were over 300 people at the funeral and many said it was very moving. Especially the boys doing his school Haka (a 'war dance' like the All Blacks do at rugby games) afterwards.

'Through the night, he gave me the second sign. I got an irresistible urge to get up and write down what he wanted to tell me. I need glasses to read and write – do you think I could find them at 2 am? No way! So I just grabbed a piece of paper and started without them. The first sentence is written in the second person (me talking about him), but from then on it is written in the first person (Logan talking about himself).

'He told me to get a trophy made in his memory; he told

me what he wanted it to look like and why: a pyramid shape similar to a driftwood sculpture he had made for his mum at Manukorihi Intermediate School which overlooks the kart track. This sculpture looks like a pair of hands reaching for the heavens.

'The top piece was to be made from Whitecliffs Rock as this is symbolic of coming home to Taranaki; the centre piece of Hinuera Stone from the quarry we had talked about going to but never made it; and the bottom piece from Oamaru Stone so South Islanders can also have a go at winning it. He even gave me the names of three sculptors for the trophy, but at the time, I only knew one of them.

'I couldn't believe it the next day when I read what I had written. I looked at the signature and said, "Boy, that looks like his writing." We couldn't find a really decent photo of him for his funeral service sheet so I was truly amazed when I took his licence out of his wallet to check the signature and found an absolutely beautiful photo of him on his school ID card behind it.

'The third sign he gave me was also on that same morning. I was looking out the kitchen window at a plant that was in dire need of attention when the window cracked right in front of my eyes! That was spooky! I have since found out through a reading that he didn't mean to make it break, he only wanted me to look at the plant!

'The fourth sign was a plant, a calendula. I deadheaded it and just as I was about to pick up the trimmings to put them in the bin, I noticed a perfectly formed flower growing out of one of the dead heads. A friend of mine has been growing flowers commercially for over twenty years and never seen anything like that before.

'At work, I phoned the local paper and asked for a particular photographer to go and take photos of it. He agreed and rang my son, Ewen, and told him to put it in some water. I had put the flower up by Logan's trophy but when the photographer got there, the flower had wilted really badly. He took some photos anyway and told Ewen to cut off the end and put it back in the water to see if it perked up. Ewen and Adrian (the photographer) took it to the sink, Ewen tipped the flower and the water out of the film case it was in and put the case in the sink. He trimmed the end of the flower. He went to refill the case with water ... and it was already full!

'The flower perked up to perfection, the previously almost brown seed head turned bright green again and Adrian got a couple of really perfect shots of it. Adrian asked why I had asked for him in person. I said I didn't know. At the time, his camera took sixteen megapixel photos which was really good then, as all the other photographers only had two megapixel cameras, so his was at least eight times better than theirs.

'I don't know if you know much about homeopathy but calendula is a flower whose oil is used to heal wounds.

'He has also given me other signs, like winding back the seat in the car I had bought for him, but only if I leave it unlocked. This has happened many times. Because he was so tall this was the only way he could fit in the car!

'I had a reading from a medium over the Christmas break and my son came through thick and strong. The psychic told me he was riding his bike and it felt like he was flying like a bird, then suddenly he realized the bike was no longer under him and he just sort of kept going. He told me there was no pain; he just looked like he was asleep when we saw him at the accident scene. The crash investigator said when he hit the concrete driveway he was barely doing thirty kph. There were no broken bones and no major injuries. His autopsy found him to be perfectly healthy. He just clonked his head in the wrong place which was such a tragedy for someone so young and just starting to go places. He'd begun his first full-time job only two days before the accident.

'Geez, I miss him. So does Eunice, his mum. She would dearly love contact from him. I have said she is too closed at the moment; he will come through when she is ready for him. We have our granddaughter, Tiana, living with us also. She used to call Logan Dada, they did everything together. She also misses him terribly. We had a motorbike stop and rev outside our house recently, and the first thing she said was "Dada" and headed for the door. Eunice burst into tears as you could imagine.'

Grief is so difficult but these experiences do help just a little. Colin sent me the photograph of the calendula flower and I had never seen anything like it. One flower grew right out of the head of another one. It was very strange. God bless you, Logan.

Here is Michelle's story.

Dramatic Display!

'My father died in 1998 from a massive heart attack aged forty-eight, just one day before he was due to have a double heart bypass. Needless to say my life fell apart on that day! Pain and heartache followed in those dark days after his death. I was praying all the time for him to visit me, to let me know he was with me.

'A few nights went by, but nothing happened until the fourth night. Everything was normal; my partner went out into the kitchen to get me a drink. Not bothering to put the light on he turned from the glass on the sideboard to the fridge, and as he did this he heard the glass move. Turning back he saw the glass hovering about an inch above the surface. With that he shot into the living room as white as a sheet; it really shocked him, especially as he was a sceptic. I found it comforting because I knew it was my dad. Anyway, when we finally went up to bed that night I prayed as I did every other night for a sign, for some tiny shred of comfort in my hour of need.

'My partner fell into his usual deep sleep, but I was finding it hard to sleep. As I closed my eyes and tried to relax I suddenly felt I wasn't alone. I wasn't anxious, in fact I was relieved. I opened my eyes but saw nothing, but then from the tips of my toes upwards I felt this heavy weight on me. It was the feeling of someone trying to hug me, it was an amazing experience and gave me hope and refreshed my slipping faith.

'I don't know how to explain how I knew it was my dad but I know for sure it was, maybe it was the weight. I don't know but dad, if you can see this, thank you for taking the time to say goodbye and I love you.'

Note from Jacky – As I was writing up this entry, I had the strangest feeling that I was not alone, and when I got to this line a shiver went right through my body! I wrote to Michelle to let her know that I felt her father was watching over me as I edited her story.

Michelle continues: 'The feeling was almost like I was paralysed from head to foot for a short space of time, but the love and warmth I felt at the same time stopped me from being scared in the slightest.

'The next morning my five year old son, who was very close to his grandad, came into my bedroom and told me that grandad came to see him that night, and he was smiling and waving to him.

'My son also saw lots of little children playing around his grandad's feet. We have lost quite a few babies and young children in our large family so it made perfect sense to me. It convinced me that in fact my father had been with us all that night – why would a small boy make up something like that? He wouldn't know to put small details like the children playing around my father into a made up story.'

I'm sure you're right, Michelle. Here is another story.

Just Like Heaven

'Like so many, I had undeniable proof of my family's existence on the other side, and although I tried to contact them myself, I couldn't, as I always start feeling uncomfortable.

'I have my own lake and houses for different things in my visualizations (in my meditations). It was hard work creating it in my mind, but now I love relaxing like that.

'In my mind, I went to my lake and imagined all of my closest relatives sitting in the garden on the other side of the lake. I could just see them. I examined how I felt about it, and realized I didn't really want to get any closer because I was scared. In my mind I had an image of zombies, and I realized that there was still residue of the "when you're dead you're dead" thinking in my mind.

'I carried on doing this visualization for a week or so, and gradually I felt more at ease. Then I started craving to be in their company. They were just hanging around, laughing and joking, and ignoring me, but they were aware of me. They were patient. Finally, when I was ready, I ran to them and they hugged me and I sat down there on the garden bench with them just chatting around me; it was nice and cosy.

'That night, my grandmother came to me in my dreams, twice. Each time she met me in one of my dreams she gave me a lilac tissue. I understood that was to help me remember I saw her. She looked over at the baby (my baby) I was feeding in my dream, and cooed over him for a moment. She said to me, "I came to see the little one," and she was gone.'

We've talked about the more common experiences of smelling flowers, perfume and tobacco, but this story was a little different. I thought it was fun so I decided to include it here. Lyn's Mum brought her the smell of chocolate!

Just Like Chocolate

'I went into our kitchen and the room was filled with the aroma of chocolates and we don't have any chocolate of any kind here at present.

'Ken was in another room at the far end of the house and I called out to him, "Have you been using anything with chocolate in it in the kitchen?"

'He said, "No. Why?"

'I said, "Because the kitchen is filled with the smell of chocolate."

'"Do you associate chocolates with anyone?"

'"Mum. She's the only person. When I went on dates, they used to bring me lovely boxes of Winning Post Chocolates and a corsage to pin on my dress. I used to give the boxes of chocolates to Mum."

'I suddenly realized the aroma was the smell of the old Winning Post Chocolates which are no longer made. The boxes they came in held the lovely aroma for ages after they were empty. I can't prove it, but I believe my mother visited us just prior to this Mother's Day and she brought me a Heavenly gift of Winning Post Chocolates for old time's sake.

'Then there was my old friend Peter ... he has contacted me

since in dreams, telling me things he felt I should know, bringing me touching gifts such as a single rose whose fragrant perfume I could actually smell!'

Some relatives and friends seem to bring us spiritual 'gifts' of contact, over and over again.

VJ seems to have experienced so many phenomena – she almost handed me a shopping list! She was worried that she might be a little crazy but I was easily able to reassure her she was not going mad.

She told me, 'I have clear visions during my sleep with visitations from loved ones … I have heard footsteps at night and felt that it was a warning sign, and a relative passed away the next day. Objects have moved in my house and office, I have had strange computer complications, and white doves have formed out of snow, sitting in my front yard tree!'

She felt that the smell of smoke was a loved one joining them in the car one day.

Smells Familiar…

'I lost a close friend to cancer last year and I feel she tries to contact me. I was driving with my three children and all of a sudden I could smell cigarette smoke. I thought I was losing it … all the windows in the car were up and nobody in my family smokes. Then my children told me that they were smelling smoke and they were questioning where it was coming from.

There was no explanation. Within a few minutes it was gone.

'My nine year old daughter thought it was the full moon doing weird things! I knew it was a loved one ... my friend or grandparents. I sensed it was my friend because she always complimented me on my skills as a good mom. I was taking my son to hockey practice and the girls wanted to join us.'

Another day, another family, and another smell …

Grandma Still Baking

'It was a beautiful Sunday afternoon. My parents, children and I decided to go for a Sunday drive to a nearby shopping mall. After picking up my parents, I could smell coconut. It was a strong odour and definitely coconut, but nobody else in the van said anything, so I just ignored the smell.

'On the way home from the outing, the smell returned. It lasted a little longer (and stronger) and this time I asked everyone in the van if they could smell anything. I asked Mom if she had purchased coconut perfume! Everyone asked me what I was talking about. Again, I questioned them if they could smell anything, and they all said no. I asked Mom if she knew anybody that liked coconut. Without hesitation, she said my grandmother! She said that Grandma loved coconut and would bake with it all the time. I never knew this. I was very close to Grandma and miss her greatly.

'My Mom, Grandma and I would go shopping together all the time, and when my mother asked me about the coconut

I told her that I could smell it on the way to and from our trip. Mum just smiled knowingly and said that Grandma probably went shopping with us today too!'

Rosemary's grandfather made himself known in his own special way.

More Tobacco...

'After my grandfather's death I would frequently smell his tobacco (he smoked Condor pipe tobacco) at my parent's house shortly before my grandmother came to visit and occasionally at other times as well. So did my brother, who usually has an appalling sense of smell and is generally not very believing of psychic phenomena.'

Andrea smelt the presence of her father – that certain something which is sometimes hard to define!

I Know That Smell!

'Last year my father died. This particular day, my husband and I went to the chapel of rest, yet as I got into the car, I immediately knew my dad was with me. (My husband doesn't believe in this sort of thing.) During the two-to-three-minute drive, I could smell my dad to my left. The smell was so strong. I turned my head to the right and there was nothing there. I asked my husband if he could smell him, but he couldn't.

'I kept sniffing, and laughing, and repeating to my husband, "Can you smell him?" As we stopped the car my husband opened the car door and then put his head back in. He was laughing now and said, "I can smell him!"

'I am convinced that my dad was in the car with us, to let me know that he was okay, and my husband (previously a non-believer) now believes in life after death.'

Lesley has experienced an assortment of phenomena too. She has learnt to 'tune in' to her spirit friends.

Lots of Reassurance

'My grandmother died ten years ago and her death was quite a shock to me as she was the first person in my life to die, and I was only fourteen at the time. I went to say goodbye to her the day before her funeral. I wanted to go and kiss her on the head but I was too afraid to go up to her so instead all I could do was look at her and leave the room. I felt really bad about this up until about a week after her funeral when I was in the car with a friend and we were listening to the radio ... I can't remember what it was we were listening to but the host mentioned the name Grace which was my grandmother's name. At that time I suddenly smelt her, I mean I smelt her perfume that she always wore, and remember feeling all warm and safe knowing that she understood about why I hadn't kissed her goodbye.

'I got over her death quite quickly because I knew she was

well and happy and although I missed her and still do, I don't feel bad. Since then I have lost six family members, some very close to me and others who weren't but I know that a part of them is still here.

'When I am upset I feel a warm weight on my shoulder and I know in my heart who is there. Most of the time it's my grandfather or my aunt who I was also very close to. Sometimes I have seen their shadows when it isn't very light, even down to the perm my grandmother had! So for me, I know they are all still around. Even though we miss the people who have left us, a part of them will always be watching over us. I strongly believe this because I've seen them and smelt them and also felt them.'

Angelic Comfort

Many people tell me about their angel stories. Sometimes our loved ones are escorted back for a visit by an angel or a being of light.

Sheila's story is amazing. She felt her angel come to her in a time of need, which was explained later by her close friend Todd.

Cleansed by My Guardian

'Near April 2000, life was getting really hard and confusing for my family. My husband and I were hitting hard times, which was unusual really. Life was getting so hard and confusing, and it seemed as if all of life's aches and pains were catching up with me. Upon the advice of others, I sought medical help, and was given medication. This just seemed to compound the pain more and more. I found myself crying every day; I truly had never felt so lost and alone, even when I was with my family.

'One night, my husband and I were having a heart-to-heart talk, and although I did feel somewhat better, I knew there was more that I needed. It was just going to be a matter of me being able to figure out what was wrong, and how to get over it. I decided to get up and get some water, and walked from the den to the dining room. It was at this point that I began feeling beside myself, or not in myself. I was almost dizzy, very warm, very cold all at the same time. I was unsure of what was happening to me. I couldn't control my feet, my thoughts, my emotions, or anything else. I noticed my vision seemed odd, it was dark in the room, yet there seemed to be some bare essence of light from afar. I began tingling all over; this sensation was unreal, and the tingling was incredibly strong. I began to wonder if I was going to faint.

'Then, through the darkness, there was this light, which kept coming closer and closer. It was a beautiful light, one that I had never seen. It felt as though this light contained the most warmth I had ever felt. The light was beginning to completely fill the room – it was radiating all the way through the room, to me. It was really so breathtaking. As I felt the light coming closer, I was surprised to notice my feet were still moving forward. I hadn't even felt them!

'Before I could even grasp this, I began seeing a figure form out of the light. As the light moved closer still, she seemed to become more defined. I could see her figure, but was unsure of what I was seeing. I remember rubbing my eyes; I remember that feeling as if it was the hardest thing to do, as I felt little to no control over my own limbs. The figure came closer to me, and I felt like I was connected to her. I noticed I could see her dress, I could see her face, I could see all about her, yet she was not like me. She was almost transparent, almost a greyish white. I couldn't see through her, but I know she was not a solid human form. I was in awe at the sight of her. She began moving closer and closer to me, as I was actually doing the same, moving closer and closer to her. It was as if there was this unbelievably strong magnet pulling us to each other.

'I can remember feeling as if I didn't know how I was even functioning! The closer we got to each other, the warmer and safer I felt. I would not have moved away from her for anything. A feeling of peace began to wash over me, a feeling of total and complete love, understanding, and acceptance. As we stood face to face, I felt her energy, and it was so strong. I felt the warmth from her, I felt love. I felt safe. All at once it was as if all God's love was shown to me.

'I hardly understood what was going on, yet at the same time, somehow, I knew exactly what was happening. We began to embrace, and as we did this, we seemed to move into one another, as if we were passing through each other. I felt her energy, her light, as it flowed all the way through me, cleansing me. Every part of me felt this energy within me. I felt like I was standing within her light, as if I, too, were of this light. It felt so unbelievably good. I began to feel as if so many things were just falling away from me, as if there was no more hurt or pain or sadness within me. I felt as if I had been cleansed completely. I felt relief. I felt ease. I felt good! I never heard her say a word, yet I know she was reminding me of God's love.

'At this point, I felt her leaving; she was actually passing through me. The light began to fade, the warmth began to wane. I didn't want this to end, I didn't want to be out there, I wanted to be with her and then I began to feel normal again and the room went back to darkness, and the light faded and faded until it was no longer visible.

'It was at this point that I discovered what it would feel like to truly be alone, or without God's love. I stood there, not knowing what to do, or what to think. I held tightly to the feeling I had felt when she was with me. I felt rejuvenated. This was really a new feeling for me. I didn't know what to do or how to feel or how to react. I was only sure I wanted her back!

'Somehow I knew there was a reason for the visit, although I was unsure of why. Not long after that, Todd, my favourite family member, passed from this world. He and I had been so close, we always knew we were soul family, and that we had been and would be together more. His death would have surely been more than I could have handled at that time in my life … if not for the visit from my angel, whom I now call Seren.

'On the day of his death, Todd came to visit me. He told

me one night in dreamtime, that the visit with my angel was what had allowed me to release all of life's pains. It was in a sense to cleanse me, so that I could carry on from there with much less inside to colour my actions. Here I am a little more than a year later, and I have had the pleasure of always feeling my angel near; she always holds me from behind, when things are just too much for me as a human to handle.

'I had the pleasure of Todd's guidance as well. I have been blessed by this event in more ways than anyone can guess. Forever, I shall be grateful and thankful for God's love and actions in my life! I have been truly changed, and awakened. For this I am eternally thankful!'

I have several similar stories on my files. I myself experienced this feeling of 'unbelievable bliss' after I went through a difficult time in my own life. Just when you think you can't go on, and that you are all alone, there it is. In my own experience, I didn't see a whole figure but felt myself lifted up in the air by a giant pair of hands … it wasn't as scary as it seems! As I was lifted higher and higher I could feel my body healed with waves of the most powerful love, God's love. I was aware of the room around me but at the same time, aware that I was also somewhere else, and afterwards I felt whole again, cleansed from my worries and strong enough to cope with whatever life brought my way. Like Shelia, I shall never forget my experience.

Life can certainly bring us 'challenges' which at times

seem more than we can bear. After the loss of a baby it is hard to imagine any comfort at all, but Samantha felt a magical, loving touch which she believed was from her angel, after the loss of her own child.

When I Needed You the Most

'During her funeral service I was inconsolable. I didn't know how I was going to make it. I had my head bowed and my face buried in my hands. The pastor was talking about McKenzie, and I just felt so hopeless and lost. As I sobbed, I felt someone kneel in front of me and place their hands on my hands. And instant peace fell over me. I immediately stopped crying. I could picture McKenzie healthy, without pain, playing with all the other baby angels in Heaven.

'I opened my eyes expecting to see a concerned family member or friend trying to console me, but no one was there. I believe it was my Guardian Angel, giving me a glimpse of hope in my darkest hour. Yes, I do believe in angels. In my life, I have been blessed by two of them.'

How inventive can our spiritual friends be? What falls into the category of 'an official visit' or what makes something 'a scientifically proven communication?' Few of the anecdotes included in this book would stand up to our current scientific testing – the very nature of the experience makes it hard to explain and understand, let alone test.

It's not so long ago that we believed the earth to be flat.

Scientifically, we couldn't prove that it was round . . . not then at least. Now, of course, we can see the earth as a whole from space and we know that it was round the whole time. As a race, our belief system is based very much on what we see, hear, feel and smell. If we can touch it, it's real . . . or is it?

Jim's story was unusual and very special. He even sent me a photograph of his 'spiritual gift'.

Gift from Mum

'I had a session with a medium a week ago. It has really made me think about things differently. The medium, Becky, communicated with my mother who passed away in 1996. Many things that came from that session were amazingly accurate to say the least.

'One of the things that she told me had to do with my house. She mentioned a retaining wall, some brick and something that needed to be painted. I told her at that time that I had a retaining wall running along my backyard, but it was treated lumber and wouldn't need to be painted and I had just added a brick edging to that corner.

'I hadn't noticed before but in that corner is a cement statue of my mother's that I brought to my house. It's a white statue of the Blessed Virgin and then I remembered, I had mentioned to my wife a week or two before the session about painting the statue with flesh tones and maybe a blue gown to make it look nicer!

'Another thing that came to Becky from my mother, was that

she wanted me to plant a rosebush in my yard. My mother always had roses, so naturally I got busy and planted two rose bushes in the corner. I put the statue there, along with a little statue of an angel and a brass plaque that reads My Gardening Angel. As I was finishing my mother's corner by spreading the stone to even it out near the edging, a stone rolled out onto the grass. The stone blew me away as it lay in the grass ... it was heart shaped. I'm not really an emotional person, but this really was something. I kept the stone!'

Debbie's husband wins my perseverance award. His amazing attempts at communication went on and on.

Still Here ... and Then Here Again

'There are so many ways that my husband communicates with me. I think he tried everything he could learn. On Valentine's Day, I found myself in uncontrollable tears. We had had a snow storm the night before and I just struggled through the day. When I went to shower after clearing my driveway, I just started crying. What triggered the tears? I turned around to reach for the soap dispenser and it was dispensing soap without my help and I hadn't even touched it!

'It reminded me of some of the little things he would do when he was alive, like leave notes for me to find. I didn't go to work that day (thank goodness I had lots of vacation time).

'Later in the day, I ventured out and took a white rose to the site of his grave. To get there I had to walk through snowdrifts up to my knees. That night when I went to bed, I closed my eyes and immediately saw a bouquet of roses which then changed to a bouquet of mixed flowers. I realized this was my spiritual gift from my husband and my son.

'A week later, the most awesome thing happened. I had gone to bed. The dogs were all snuggled in. I turned off the lights and the TV then laid my head down. About that time, the dogs started to bark. Of course, I got up and turned the lights on, checked the house and calmed the dogs down. I went back to bed and turned the lights off. Immediately, the largest heart I ever saw appeared over my bed. It lasted only a few seconds but long enough for me to sit in awe.'

Debbie felt that her husband worked alongside her for many months and instilled knowledge which she hadn't previously had, as well as acting as a sort of 'guardian angel' for her.

'Just before his death, we adopted two llamas. Of course, we had to prepare for them. We took our old sheep shelter and turned it into a sixteen-foot barn, however, my husband never had a chance to finish applying the shingles to the roof. I'm not sure how I managed but somehow, I was able to finish the barn roof and I always felt that he had somehow passed me the knowledge.

'Then, I had to replace the furnace before fall. However, the doorway I needed to move the old furnace through didn't have any steps. So, I built a four-foot-square deck. It was as if he told me how to use the electric mitre saw to cut all my lumber, perfectly. The knowledge was suddenly there.

'Before the new furnace was installed, the weather did turn

> cold so I had to use the wood stove for heat. One night, I went to bed, with the stove dampened down for the night. The next morning, none of the wood had burned. When I relit the stove, I immediately had a chimney fire and I feel sure that he saved my life and home by putting the fire out while I slept.'

Had the dogs sensed their master in the house when he brought the heart? Had he been able to put out the stove? We'll never know but when little coincidences string together like this you have to wonder.

Susan had a gift in the shape of a candle flame, she told me, 'The candle made a heart shape in pink and I know who sent that, dad always sends hearts!' Of course, hearts, like my 'x' for love in the early chapters are common enough signs in life and afterlife … those simple 'I love you' messages which they want to bring us, over and over again.

Andrea told me a story about her sister.

Gift of Flowers

> 'My sister brought flowers for my dad's funeral and took them straight home from the shop. My aunty and sister were having a cup of tea, when one of the flowers fell out of the wreath. She said that the flower just fell to the floor as they were drinking their tea. She was going to put the flower back into the wreath, but couldn't find where it had come from. She was convinced that my dad had taken it out and, dropped it to the floor to let them know he was there.'

This story is nice because more than one person was in the room at the time of the experience. Often we are the only ones that seem to be aware though, even in a room full of people. And of course, it can be hard to explain to someone else. Adam's sister and a couple of her friends celebrated their thirtieth birthdays around the same time, so a party was held for all of them.

Join the Party

'During the course of the evening I felt the presence of both my dad and my mum (sadly she had passed away the previous year). I could feel them all round me and in my mind's eye I could see them holding hands and smiling. They were so happy it was a wonderful feeling.

'I didn't receive another visit until 1998 when my baby daughter was born. My daughter had a little bit of a difficult birth and so had to spend a couple of days in the special baby care unit for observation. Soon after that she was allowed to join me – I had a room to myself. It was in the afternoon and I was standing at the end of the short corridor that leads into the room. I felt a wonderful feeling of happiness and I could feel my parents standing in the doorway holding hands. It was a really special time.

'Only a couple of days ago my dad visited me again. It happened to be on the anniversary of his death and the first time he has visited me on this date. I was at work and standing in the print room by myself when I had that good feeling again. I saw my dad standing next to me with a big smile on his face, it was wonderful.

'I decided to email my sister to tell her what had happened, and she told me that she'd had a strange coincidence of her own that day. She emailed me back to tell me she had seen her old counsellor at the train station, and that previously she had talked to her a lot about dad. It was strange that she hadn't seen her in a year, and now she saw her on his anniversary.

'To my knowledge she has never felt the presence of our parents sadly. It's hard to share with someone and I feel genuinely lucky to have these visits and I don't feel that I'm any more spiritual than the next person.'

Yes, it can be hard to share these experiences with others, especially when there is little for another person to grasp. How do you explain 'a feeling'?

Kate's Dad was another persistent visitor.

If at First You Don't Succeed…

'My dad died when I was eighteen. Over the last two or three years I've had contact with him in various ways, like flickering lights, and songs on the radio at significant times. I feel him holding my hand frequently.

'Last year I was breaking up with my partner and feeling very low. I could feel a breeze around me and suddenly could smell my dad's pipe smoke, then felt him holding my hands. I felt very calm and could feel my dad very close to me.

'As it was late at night I went upstairs to bed but I could still smell his pipe smoke for two or three hours afterwards. Whilst I was getting my bag ready for work, I put my hand in the front pocket and pulled out a big old penny which I didn't even know was there. As I held the penny, I could feel him with me.

'Now, whenever I feel low I sit and hold the penny, which makes me feel safe and secure. Wherever I go, it goes. I can often hear my dad guiding me and giving me visual signs too.'

The most persistent communicator ever was (and still is) Anne (see the next chapter). She visited lots of friends and family members and tested several communication methods over many months. Anne has her own chapter.

Often, when our loved ones work so hard, I believe it has as much to do with their own grief as ours. Although I believe that we all have 'our time', there are occasions when people pass so quickly, or in unforeseen accidents, that their souls are in a short-term state of confusion. One story even involved the deceased having to be told that they had died!

Having said all of that, it is far more common for our loved ones to be whisked away to their new heavenly home by angels, guides or deceased loved ones. They can be having so much fun that they might not immediately be aware that we are grieving for them. Time in the heavenly realms is very different to time in our world.

The type and variety of experience seems only limited by our loved ones' imaginations. It's great when a professional psychic confirms our experiences. Here is what Adele told me.

Hide and Seek

'I had been quite ill with depression after my mother died suddenly. Almost immediately I began to sense her presence and believed I "heard" her talking to me. A little while later I visited a psychic fair and a reader told me what I thought my mother had said, thereby confirming my suspicions!

'Time passed by and the mundane world sort of took over, then one day after I had been looking for my mother's jewellery for many days, it turned up right in front of my eyes!'

How long do our loved ones stay around after they pass over? Do they visit at once and briefly before moving on for good, or do they take many years to get used to their new homes before they are ready to see us again? Maybe they never stop visiting and make their presence known for years and years. Of course, we know that all of these are correct.

Patrick told me he still feels his soul mate around him all the time, even though she passed away over ten years ago.

Soul Mate

'I feel her energy, and get "goosebumps" and tingling whenever I am near her photograph. I see a rainbow of colour around her photograph, and I hear her call my name in my head. I actually see specks and sparkles of white light around me all the time, and I constantly get signs like songs, and personal things suddenly happen!'

He had a theory about the whole thing which he felt was an understanding brought about by his contact with his soul mate.

'Most people are unaware and not paying attention to subtle signs and coincidences which are happening all around them. Our connections go far beyond our time in this physical world and we have spirits close to us who we may have never met in this lifetime. This is only a very small part of the whole picture!'

I agree with Patrick. Most of us are not aware of what goes on under our very noses!

Jill Wellington (author of the novel *Fireworks*, published by Stargate Press) emailed me one of her many stories.

Taking Dictation from Friends on the Other Side

'My mom and I were talking before I left for my friend Ann's funeral in Canada and we were discussing my mom's friend who had recently lost her husband. The light kept popping on in the bedroom in the middle of the night and this friend thought it was her dead husband saying hello. We thought that was neat.

'I drove with the kids to stay with my brother and his wife Joyce in Ann's house (Ann was Joyce's mother) after the funeral. Joyce put me in Ann's room which was spooky because all her personal things were still in place like she would return at any time. That night I was awakened from a deep sleep at three in the morning by a bright light. I was shaken when I opened my eyes and was almost blinded by the bedside light which was suddenly on! I knew immediately Ann had turned on the light ... just as Mom and I discussed only days earlier. That is why it scared me so much, because I knew!

'I quickly shut off the lamp and laid back down with my eyes squeezed shut. I was afraid I would see Ann! Then I got a hold of myself, and realized she needed to communicate with me. So I sat up in bed and turned on the light and said to her, "Dearest Ann, if you need to speak to me I am willing." Then a list started tumbling into my mind ... I quickly grabbed a pad of paper off her beside table and got a pen out of my purse and wrote it down.

'My sister-in-law is not into this stuff at all, but she listened when I read her the list. I don't know what she ever did with it though, or if she took any notice – I just passed on the message, which is what I felt I must do.'

Terri and her aunt Lois wrote to me for advice about how

they might contact their grandmother. They had earlier written with regard to another incident and they wondered if this had been a spirit contact.

Is This Her?

'My grandmother "Chee-Chee" passed away on 22 July 1996 and I was very close to her, as was my aunt Lois. My aunt and I had a hard time with her passing and still longed for her, so it was no coincidence when we bumped into each other at the cemetery one day. I had placed an angel cherub statue at the grave site over a year ago, and my aunt loved it. In the cherub's hand was a small bird (my grandmother was very fond of birds), but when we got to the grave side the cherub was missing, and we were both very upset.

'We spent a lot of time combing through the trash looking for the cherub because even though it had no monetary worth it meant a lot to us. We couldn't find it but as we were walking to our cars I turned around, although I still don't know why. I happened to notice a red cardinal bird sitting in a tree, way up high in the branches, but the more I looked at the red bird I realized the bird was not real but artificial. As my eyes became clearer I saw the cherub nestled back on the same branch, as if it were placed there for us to find it. No one knew we were at this site and in this particular part of the church yard. We were in shock, and I started crying. I actually had to climb up the tree to get the cherub out.

'This area of the churchyard was deserted and full of trash

(dead flowers and broken vases). When I got the cherub out of the tree we noticed the little bird in her hand was missing! It was almost as if the artificial bird turned into a real bird to show us where the cherub was sitting! We both feel my grandmother had put the cherub in the tree for us to find because we were so upset to find it missing.'

Many people have success with spiritual visitations or receiving loving communication by praying and actually asking their loved ones to appear to them or give them a sign. Later, Terri wrote to me again and asked me how they might get another sign so that they would know for sure and I suggested that they pray.

Terri wrote to me later to share their experience.

...Yes It Is!

'The first anniversary of our earlier experience was 24 March. My aunt and I started to pray and talk to my grandmother before our planned meeting back at the cemetery. I was thinking of my grandmother and glancing at her photograph like you suggested, then as I drove along the song "Thank You" by Dido came on the radio. At exactly that moment I came to an overpass, and glanced up just in time to see a message written on the overpass that said "I LOVE YOU L xxx T". The word "love" was in the shape of a heart. Well, my name is Terri and my aunt's name is Lois! I turned my car around and I had my digital camera with me so I took a photograph. You can imagine that I was so excited and I could not wait to meet my aunt. We both believe it was another sign from my grandmother.

'It seemed too much of a coincidence to be the initials of our first names. I have travelled that road hundreds of times and have never noticed it before. The feeling just hit me that that was what we were looking for.

'We also believe she is with us every day and always! I don't believe we just die and go away forever, but there is an "afterlife", or heaven. I believe our sprits do live on and who is to say that's not the truth? Nobody really knows. That's why they leave signs all around us. We just need to be open to them. I think that everybody has that ability to see them but some just choose not to.'

And of course Terri also sent me the photograph as proof!

How can you tell when an experience is an afterlife contact? Sometimes the contact is subtle, and sometimes not so subtle. Many times the contact comes as a result of a deep inner need, to assist us with our grief or even to save a life. Our loved ones are always in our hearts … and often at our parties! Remember to invite your loved ones into your life – both in this life and the next. You can be sure that if they can be there, they certainly will.

CHAPTER 12

Love from Anne

... one spirit's personal role in proving life after death to her family and friends

Do not stand at my grave and weep,
I am not there, I do not sleep...

Mary E Frye

'Annie' was my sister's beloved friend. Her death at a very young fifty-three was a great shock to her family and friends. It seemed that the death was a shock to Anne herself who spent much of the next few months visiting her loved ones – and even me! My sister told me about their last visit together before she passed over.

> 'We spent an evening together, two couples eating a curry! We drank a lot of wine, we laughed a lot and had fun like long-term friends do. We have known each other for many years and been through so many things together. It was a wonderful night, just four friends having a laugh together.

'Anne's partner David (who I had worked with, for over twenty years) and I spent the evening telling jokes as always. My partner Neil and Anne talked about more sensible things, and pretended not to laugh at the dirty jokes as they always did. It was a lovely evening, just lovely.

'We stayed the night in their beautiful guest bedroom. I remember Anne bringing us a cup of tea in bed! David was going to cook us breakfast but I was disappointed because my partner wanted to go home to see his son from his first marriage. I always regretted not staying for breakfast and he still feels guilty that we left early. I remember her standing at the door waving us goodbye – it was the last time I saw her conscious.

'The next time I saw her, she was in hospital on a ventilator. She looked so glamorous and had some pretty earrings in, and her gorgeous shiny blonde hair was lying on the pillow. Anne was truly peaceful and I chatted to her and held her hand, but she was heavily sedated. It reminded me of when my dear old dad was in a coma. He'd had a brain haemorrhage but as he made such a dramatic recovery, I suppose I thought ... we all thought, that Anne would make it too. But she didn't. Her death was so unexpected.

'I don't want to go into details, I can't, but it wasn't as if she had been ill. It was so quick, so unexpected. Something happened in her brain and she just collapsed and never came to. Everyone that knew her was in deep shock. It was unbelievable. She was so well known in our little village and everyone loved her. Anne was the receptionist in our local village dental surgery and she always had a good word to say to everyone. She was the sort of person who always remembered what you had talked about the last time she saw you. Then she'd ask you about how you'd got on or how your family was. She remembered everyone's names ... It was just such an awful time and how we got through the funeral I'll never know.

'But then she started to show us that she was around – perhaps she was aware of how badly we were all coping? It was a while after the funeral when strange things started happening. Shortly before she died, she had given me her garden "bird bath", and every day after she died, I used to watch a single white dove come down to the bird bath and stare at me through the window. I often wondered if it was her.

'I shared my experience with her partner David and he started to tell me about his own experiences. One day, he told me, he could hear her in the house and didn't understand what was happening. He told me, "I felt that I must be imagining it, but I know I heard her pottering about upstairs."

'When his daughter came to the house a few days later, she admitted that she'd heard it too. At one point they wondered if there was an intruder in the house, but there was no one there.

'On another occasion he heard the post drop onto the mat at the front door, just a few feet away. He got up to collect the post, but again, there was nothing there. A few moments later, he heard it again and once more walked to the door to discover that there was still no post!

'Incredibly, at that moment, the front door burst open! The dog started wagging her tail and getting really excited – but there was still no one at the door! David told me, "That was Anne's greeting, the dog only ever got excited like that when Anne came home."

'The front door had never come open like that before – there is no way that it could do that! Could it?

'Recently David walked to the local shop to pick up some groceries. When he returned he was confused to discover that his keys were missing and walked all the way back to the shop – retracing his steps trying to see if he had dropped them on the way. He even went into the shop to see if he had left them behind. When he got back to the house, a neighbour and a passer-by were both helping him look for the keys around the house when they noticed that the keys were on the inside of the door, with the door locked from the inside! It wasn't the sort of door that you could just pull to. It has to be actually locked. Even the neighbour said to him, "How did that happen – that was impossible!" It was impossible – but still it had happened.

'One day David told me he had been sitting on the patio thinking about Anne. He looked up into the sky and a cloud changed into the shape of her image. When he told me about it he said, "You'll never guess what's happened now!" I think it has been hard for him to understand what is happening because he is a very sceptical person. He tells me because I am sympathetic and believe what he is saying. We had a joke about watching *The Lion King* where Simba's dad appeared to Simba in a cloud!

'This week, he told me about a conversation he'd had with his daughter.

'They were joking about a visit they'd received from three of Anne's friends after they'd called to view a memorial bench which had been erected in her honour. Lizzy, David's daughter had teased her dad about one of the friends being single and joked about a possible future relationship with this attractive woman, wondering if Anne would approve of such a relationship. They laughed off the idea.

'Later, whilst watching TV, they noticed a car number plate seemed to keep flashing up on the screen. The letters formed this woman's name! It seemed significant enough to mention!'

Had Anne instigated the image or had she put the original idea into their heads, knowing the clip, confirming her plan would appear on the show later on? Who knows. It was yet another strange coincidence. Was the woman going to be 'the one'? Possibly not, but it may have meant that Anne was listening in on the conversation anyway.

Family and friends continued to receive visits from Anne in dreams. In fact, I myself had a dream visitation. I'd known Anne for many years, and I knew she'd visited me because I'd happily share the experience with other family and friends.

I was in the middle of a boring dream. In fact, the dream was in a car park and the colours were very dull. Suddenly I turned round and Anne was walking towards me. The colours of the dream instantly became bright and clear. Anne looked beautiful and younger than I had ever seen her. Her clothes were very vivid, and I could even make out the texture on her pale blue sleeveless top. I rushed towards her and threw my arms around her. To be honest I think she was a little taken aback. She felt real and solid and I realized that she was dead when I said to her, 'How are you? We've missed you!'

Anne looked a little sad as she shook her head. 'I know,' she said.

We chatted for a few more moments but I don't remember what she said. I do know that she was with someone whom I was unable to make out clearly, it was a sort of 'guide' or companion. In the dream before she arrived, I was with my husband and two daughters. They seemed unaware of her visit and, in fact, were not looking in our direction at all.

The next day I told my sister who passed back the message to David. I asked specifically that the family receive the details of the top that Anne was wearing. Yes, Anne had owned a top exactly as I had described but the confirmation was for their benefit rather than mine ... I already believed it was real.

Debbie seemed a little upset. 'Why can't Anne appear to me in a dream? I was such a good friend of hers?'

I didn't have an answer. Why do spirits choose to visit one person over another? Is there a pattern or a reason we don't understand? Is one person more open than another, or is it simply that when the visit/time slot appears, maybe one person is dreaming at the appropriate moment or even asleep at the correct time? I wasn't sure, but Debbie didn't have to wait long to receive a visit of her own.

Seven months after Anne died she appeared to Debbie in a dream visitation.

'I stepped down off a tram onto flagstones, I know I was at the beach and it was at Brighton, in England. Anne appeared in front of me looking younger than she did when she'd died. I was thrilled because I realized immediately that Anne was "dead" and so knew that this was a "visit" not just a dream.

'She held out her arms. She was wearing salmon-coloured trousers, a gift for my daughter. Anne told me they were a size ten and they needed a wash, and with a slight adjustment they would fit! Strange but appropriate as Anne was always at the "nearly new" shop and was known for her "clutter", but never liked to waste anything.

'Moments later, I followed her along the seafront with another woman at my side. This woman had a "floaty" white dress and dark curly hair and I couldn't really see her face, but I felt she was a sort of guide.

'We reached the sea front and I was at the far side. The woman with the dark curly hair lay on an old rusty gate, and I couldn't get close to Anne now. There were people walking past the gate and I remember thinking it a bit odd that they didn't comment on someone lying on a gate, face down! Anne was the other side of a statue, behind the gate. In front of me I noticed a sheer drop and the sea was in the background. There was a very big man, "larger than life", with a beard, wearing a suit, standing on the beach. His legs seemed to disappear into the sand – into the white light! He was with

Anne, beckoning her to come to him. I felt she'd stayed as long as she was allowed to. He seemed to be guiding her, as if it was time to go.

'I was disappointed that she was going but I didn't want to go with her – I wanted her to be with me! She jumped off the wall and disappeared into the sand. I didn't understand who the other people were but I realized it wasn't an ordinary dream. Everything was in bright white light, and I'd remembered immediately that she was dead. The people were looking after her and I wasn't allowed to go over the gate to the other side to be with her, but that was okay.

'Then the phone rang, waking me up. It was my mother. I had difficulty concentrating on the call because I was still excited about this amazing dream. When I put the phone down it rang almost immediately and it was my sister and I was now ready to talk about what I had experienced. I'd had a few moments to go over it in my head.

'It continues to be one of very few dreams that I will remember forever. I remember every detail, what she was wearing and how she looked. I felt thrilled that she'd come to me in this way and I felt really privileged. I couldn't wait to tell David, and I knew he would be comforted to hear about my dream.'

Debbie still feels Anne around her.

'We went to a garden centre last week. They sold lots of lovely candles and beaded candle holders and I knew she would have loved them. I was thinking about her when I felt a touch on my left hand. I knew she was with us.'

Debbie's final words echo those from many of the communications that I have received from around the world.

'I think she will continue to visit me, because she's still being a good friend. I'm still very upset that she's no longer here as a physical body, but knowing that she's still around me brings me great comfort. I look forward to being with her again one day.'

As she dictated her final words to me we both sighed, and then something alerted our senses. A loud thump on the ceiling above us sounded like the dog had jumped off the bed – except the dog was lying by my side. 'We'd better go and investigate,' suggested Debbie as we cautiously crept up the stairs together.

We found nothing … which is what we expected. It seems that Anne had the last 'word' after all.

Now it was at this point that I had decided to end the chapter, but Anne had not finished. Debbie and Neil got married a while later. Anne appeared in another dream visitation wearing her 'wedding clothes', dressed as if she were ready to attend as a guest at the wedding – which I'm sure she did.

Later, Debbie remembers receiving a congratulations card with a single name on it, saying, 'Lots of love, Anne'.

Debbie knew a couple of people called Anne, and asked them if they had sent her the card, which had been delivered by hand. No one had, and she never did find out who had sent the card, but Debbie tells me she recognizes the handwriting! Strange, isn't it? Perhaps Anne had found a way of communicating once again.

As you can guess, several years later, she still continues to visit, and probably always will. We miss you Anne, God bless.

Part 3

CHAPTER 13

Our Animal Angels

Until one has loved an animal, a part of
one's soul remains unawakened.

Anatole France

You've already read about amazing afterlife contact by our loving animals, but no book about angels would be complete without mentioning our loving animals here on earth … especially our own dear pets.

Often a particular animal seems to have a mission here on earth in the very same way that we humans do. I know that is the case with my own dear cat Tigger … or Tiggy, as we usually call him.

Born to be With You

'No more cats,' said my husband for the hundredth time, but when the dreams started I knew we would have one. I dreamt of a ginger kitten that was chasing a butterfly around in the garden.

The next morning my daughter came downstairs, 'Mum, I had a funny dream last night, I dreamt we had a ginger kitten!' That was it, how many more signs did I need?

I made a few phone calls and several places had kittens but none of them were ginger. Just the same we went to have a look at some, which of course was a mistake. The first place we went I felt as if they were rushing me to choose a pet. In the end, I pointed in the direction of a small black and white female. She was very sweet and they told us we could collect her the following night.

But even before we left the building I began to cry. My husband got cross with me and decided to wait in the car whilst I filled out the paperwork. Why was I crying? Was it because I wanted to take this little kitten home now or was it because of all the cats we'd loved and lost in the past? I had no idea, but as I got back into the car, I just cried even more.

I felt so unhappy. The next day, something still felt wrong. I'd seen a shorthaired, ginger tom cat in my dream and this was a female, long haired, black and white cat – this wasn't my cat at all! There was nothing for it but to phone up the rescue centre and tell them I had changed my mind. I felt awful but this cat was waiting for another owner. I would have to look a little harder.

Then the next day I received a telephone call. A lady from another rescue centre had been trying to get hold of me and she was sorry that she'd also been away for a few days. A 'foster mum' was looking after three kittens and two of them were ginger tom cats. Would we like to go and have a look?

This sounded right! Later that day she called at the house to check we lived in an area that was safe for a kitten. After we passed the test we jumped in the car – I'd already bought a cat basket, food bowls, food and a pet carrier, so I was ready. The kittens were housed in an outside run and when we went in to see them they bit and scratched. They'd been found in the wild apparently, so were not used to humans yet. I tried to pick up all of the kittens in turn but none of them seemed interested. One of the ginger cats had an infection so that left just one ginger tom kitten and his sister, a small black female. My youngest daughter and I exchanged knowing glances. We knew which was our cat, even if he was a little frightened!

But then, something totally unexpected happened, my eldest daughter threw a fit because she wanted the smaller female. No way was my husband was having two cats, and he held his ground. What on earth was I to do? This wasn't part of the plan. Then an idea popped into my head. I asked my daughter to pick up the black kitten and if she still wanted it, we would have her instead of the ginger tom cat I had seen in my dream. All I could do was pray ...

Charlotte reached over to pick up the small ball of black fur and immediately, she clawed her way angrily up my poor daughter's body, spitting and hissing before bouncing off her shoulder, and racing to hide in the bedding area at the top of the run. Charlotte let out a yell of pain, and rather meanly, I breathed a big sigh of relief and picked up the ginger kitten and placed him in the pet carrier. We all walked silently into the carer's home to sign off on the final paperwork.

Tigger was named on the way home in the car, and for twenty-four hours he didn't leave the box we'd placed him in. But by the morning, he felt brave enough to sneak out and use the litter tray in the kitchen before jumping back into his little cardboard box. Three days later he was roaming all over the house. He was home!

Tigger settled in really well and it was obvious to everyone how he gave our old dog a new lease of life. The two of them would run around after each other, hide and then jump on each other, causing the rest of us to roar with laughter. My husband John was suffering a lot from stress at this time and it was clear that there were days when only the cat made him laugh. It was wonderful therapy.

By the summer, Tigger was a very big kitten indeed, and really rather beautiful. We'd been having a summer so warm that the only place to be during the day was lying in the shade of the house. Tigger spent most of the day asleep on the bed but by the early evening, it had cooled down and he was desperate to go outside. I never let Tigger out at night, and I resisted for three days but by the fourth night, he just sat and cried and gave me this face full of big sad eyes and I relented. What was the harm? I was going to be pottering about the garden anyway so I could easily keep my eye on him.

I floated about the garden tying up the climbing plants. Everything was growing so well and it was so pretty out in the garden, but I'd got distracted for just a moment and I couldn't see the cat.

'Tigger? Tigger?'

Tigger never went far normally, and he always came back when we called him. Something was wrong, I knew it. My heart ached, and I had a real physical pain in my stomach. Something was wrong.

'Tigger? Tigger?' Panic was beginning to build up inside. Why was I so worried, he was a cat and cats explore. He was sure to come home, I tried to reason with myself, but I knew there was a problem.

Two hours later and my sister arrived at the door. She tried to calm me by pointing out that he'd only actually been gone for a couple of hours, but I still felt anxious. By midnight he still hadn't come home so I left his bed outside and his food and tried to get to sleep. I tossed and turned in my bed all night. Every few minutes I was hanging my head out of the window, and by the morning he still hadn't arrived. I was a complete physical wreck!

Then the nightmares began. Every night I could hear Tigger in my head, it was like he was saying, 'Come and find me, come and get me ... help me ... I'm frightened.' I was aware of him digging and scratching as if he had been locked in somewhere. When, several days later we had horrific thunder storms I was pleased. Maybe, if he is shut in somewhere, the thrashing rain will get under a door and Tigger might be able to get a drink ...

Two weeks later there was no sign of him still and people reassured me with tales of how cats have returned home after being missing for days and even weeks, but I was inconsolable.

Part of my work involved me suggesting that people ask their angels for help when they are in difficulties in their life. But here I was, the 'angel lady', and it hadn't even occurred to me that this was an option, I'd just forgotten! I was grieving so hard for my little cat that I had completely forgotten to ask the angels for their help!

That night, before I went to bed, I took a notebook and wrote a message. 'Dear angels, please can you show me where Tigger is?' That night I had a dream. I could see Tigger at the other end of our village. Ironically, he was sitting outside a local school in a road that I had grown up in ... although Tigger had never lived in that house. First thing the next morning I rushed to the end of the village and began knocking on people's doors. One person suggested that I put posters up. Children, she said, would find him.

I rushed home full of hope and created some laminated posters using a photograph which showed his markings to best effect, and then rushed out and posted them up around the schools and in the local supermarket.

Another couple of days went by and although people phoned in, their sightings came to nothing. But after my dream I felt sure he was alive, so I decided to ask the angels for help again. 'Please angels, can you show me where he is again?' As you can guess, that night I had another dream and he was in the same road but this time he was sitting on a driveway. Again I rushed to the same road and this time I knocked on the door of the house I had seen him at. The owner clearly didn't like cats and closed the door fairly promptly!

By the end of the week I was struggling to sleep at night. I could still hear Tigger calling in my head but it had become weak. Was he dying? I've been through some trauma in my life but you have no idea how I felt about losing my cat. I can't begin to describe how it felt and I had no idea why my feelings for this small ball of fur were so strong, but they were.

It was now over three weeks since Tigger had gone missing and everyone around me was talking about buying another cat but I knew he was still alive somewhere. I was reading through my request to the angels and realized I had made a mistake. I had asked them to show me where he was. Why hadn't I simply asked them to bring him home to me? That night I asked again. 'Please angels, bring Tigger home to me!' Of course, you know I'm going to tell you that I had another dream! This time I heard a knock at the door. A 'man' was there and he was delivering cats home who were lost. He had a cat under each arm and one of them was Tigger! This 'man' then turned, jumped back into his car and drove away. Were the angels showing me that he would be brought home?

At breakfast my daughter couldn't wait to tell me about her dream. 'Mum, I dreamt that a lady brought Tigger home. She just drove up to the door and handed him over ...'

Later that night my sister rang. 'I know this sounds strange but Nick had a dream and he saw Tigger coming across the fields with a fox. They were friends and they had been on a great adventure ... but Tigger was on his way home!'

Was it a coincidence? Did it mean a man and a woman were bringing my cat home? Or were the angels showing me simply that we were getting him back? I was positive that he was coming home safe and sound now, but there was a problem. My husband John and I were working away from home at an exhibition that weekend and we weren't going to be around to greet him but I knew that the angels would find a way.

After we finished at the exhibition on Saturday we went out with a crowd of friends and we were sitting in the restaurant when my friend asked sadly, 'Any news of the cat?'

A big smile came across my face. 'Yes,' I said confidently, 'the angels are bringing him home to me, I had a dream.'

She looked at me sympathetically, 'In a new body?'

I laughed out loud. Did she mean that the angels were sending me my cat back as if he had reincarnated and was now in another body?

'No,' I reassured her, 'I dreamed that the angels sent someone to deliver him to my house! He'll be home any time now.'

Just at that very second, my mobile telephone rang on the table next to me. I had to excuse myself because the restaurant was too noisy for me to hear properly, so I carried the telephone outside ... it was worth standing outside in the rain.

'Hello? Is that Mrs Newcomb? I have your cat, can you come and collect him?'

'You have Tigger?'

'Yes, it's definitely him, I've seen his photograph on your poster.'

I couldn't believe it – but of course I could! I was so confident there in the restaurant ... what perfect timing.

Of course, we still had a second day at the exhibition so we were unable to pick him up personally. I had to immediately make arrangements for Tigger to be picked up by someone else – my parents were the angels that day!

We rushed home on the Sunday night and Tigger was in a bit of a state. He was so thin and his paws had turned pink. I realized with a flash of insight that I was right when I could 'see' him trapped, that he really must have been trying to dig himself out. His paws had bled so much the blood had stained his little paws. We really had made that psychic connection.

Tigger had been less than a mile from my house, and strangely, it was at a house right across a field like Nick had seen in his dream. Tigger was found shaking underneath a cherry tree. The owners were cat lovers themselves and had been visiting their new home before they were due to move into the house properly, a few weeks later. They had a cat themselves, and coincidentally he was also called Tigger! The owner had seen my poster in the local shop.

Later, a psychic told me that Tigger had been chased by a large black and white cat and got himself trapped in someone's garage. When he was finally released, he'd got lost after walking round and round. He'd walked into the field, full of crops, looking for food, but was then unable to find his way out. I have no idea if it was true but it made sense of everything.

All Tigger did for a week when he came home was eat, sleep and purr. He was home, and that is where he wanted to stay! I had to learn to trust that he would be safe when he went out again a week later, and eventually we even bought him a cat-flap so he could come and go when he wanted. Tigger never goes far now and every time we call him, he always comes right back. Never again will I doubt that psychic connection between pets and their owners because I know for sure that Tigger reached out to me in his time of need, and I never gave up hope that he was alive.

Tigger spends much of his day sitting next to me whilst I work. He has been the inspiration for many articles and often sits right on my desk or even on my keyboard. He still makes us all laugh more than anything in life – and perhaps that is the reason he is with us, to keep us all stress free? Who knows?

It's strange but I always said that one cat was plenty, but two nights ago I dreamt of another ginger tom cat. I saw him clearly and he was about five weeks old. I have told the angels that if they want me to have this new kitten they have to convince my husband personally! Will we have another cat? I'll let you know!

Pets bring special gifts to humans. Many elderly people keep a cat for company, many people's lives have been saved by their dogs. Animals certainly have a special role to play in our lives. Do you have special pets in your life?

I believe that angels often involve humans to carry out their work for them, but of course, this is the same for animals. Even the very small ones. I loved this fun story that Melanie sent me. Melanie lives in New Zealand.

Kitten to the Rescue

'I read one of your books recently, and was amazed that so many of the stories, and your personal experiences, were exactly the same as my own. I have never asked for help from my angel before, but I realized that nothing else was helping me.

'It all started about two weeks ago. I had lost a set of house, car and garage keys and I had searched and searched the house, emptied kitchen drawers, checked the settees, looked under the beds, etc. By the end of the two weeks I was beginning to get really stressed out, and felt very concerned about where they were. I went to bed and read the last chapter of your book, and decided right there and then to ask the angels to help me.

'I then went into our kitchen alone, and asked out loud to my angel, "Please, if I do have an angel, please can you help me find those keys, as I am getting so worried about where they might be." I went back into my bedroom and unbelievably our nine-month-old kitten (who does not behave like a cat at all) came walking into my bedroom carrying the keys in his mouth. I couldn't believe it, the kitten was actually bringing me the keys. I was so shocked, I began jumping up and down and got very excited!

'I ran out to my husband and his mouth just dropped open and he said, "Now that's scary!" Then I ran into our kitchen and said out loud, "Thank you so much."

'I have told numerous people about this event. Some are amazed, some look at me as if to say, "Well, if you want to believe that sort of thing." I definitely know what I believe, and it has confirmed what I always thought anyway.'

It seems that the angels made full use of their animal helper, and what a fun way for the keys to turn up. Scary? Kittens? Never!

During the course of my research I spent a great deal of time searching on the internet. This next story hit headlines all over the world.

Cat 911

Fifty-year-old Gary had a lucky escape when his cat dialled 911, the emergency help line in the US. Tommy, a ginger tom, really saved the day when owner Gary fell out of his wheelchair and was unable to call for help. Gary suffers from osteoporosis and mini strokes which make it dangerous for him to be left alone.

All is not what it seems, however, because Gary had actually taught Tommy to call for help using the emergency button on the telephone. However, it wasn't until there was a real emergency that Gary was sure Tommy would be able to react! The police say they had no other explanation as to how the emergency help lines had been alerted.

Perhaps cats are cleverer than we give them credit for … or maybe, Tommy had a little angel help!

Here's another rescue story. This one is in two parts,

and in the second part, the angels ask their doggie helper to play nurse.

Nurse Ben, the Guardian Angel Dog

'I have believed in angels for as long as I can remember. Last week I started having dreams about my daughter being hit by a car (she is only seven). In the dream she and her older brother were playing a silly road tag game. On the second night after having the same dream, I felt I had to sit her and her older brother down and explain to them to be careful on the road and to never play silly games. Once I told them, I slept soundly and never had the dream again.

'Two days later my daughter fell ill. She was sleeping a lot which is not like her. Later in the day she seemed to get worse and I was monitoring her temperature which was rising slowly. The next day she was complaining of headaches and dizziness. She was still sleeping a lot and her temperature was now 39°C, so I rang the doctor who told me to bring her straight down. After the doctor checked her over, I was told that she had tonsillitis and an ear infection as well as a fever; I was given medication for her and sent home.

'Yet even after I had given her the medication she didn't seem any better. I was getting worried as her stomach was in pain. Her temperature was still high, and she kept slipping in and out of consciousness. I checked on her but she did not recognize either me or her brother, and the sweat was just dripping off her, so I decided to call the doctor again.

'The doctor just gave me advice over the phone on how to keep her temperature down, and to ring back if she started fitting. I was seriously concerned – enough to ask the angels to watch over her whilst she was sleeping.

'That night my dog Ben started acting very weird and restless before he disappeared upstairs. I left him, thinking he had gone to my room where he sleeps at night, but to my surprise, when I went up to bed to check on the children, Ben was lying at my daughter's feet. He just refused to leave her, so I left her bedroom door ajar in case. Several times, I woke and checked on my daughter but Ben never left her side all night long and when she woke the next morning, her temperature had almost returned to normal. She has no memory of what happened and was just surprised to find Ben on her bed when she woke up. I believe Ben was protecting my daughter and keeping an eye on her. We now call him our Guardian Angel Dog!'

Dogs are very sensitive to human illness, as are other pets. I'm sure that Ben was carrying out his angelic orders, and a good job he did, too.

Jane tells me that the stranger that protected her was a dog.

Black Labrador Stands Guard

'My husband and I went to Corfu a few years ago on holiday. Whilst we were there, there was a small pack of dogs consisting of one bitch and about four other dogs.

'These dogs were a pest because they liked human contact and would very often follow myself and my husband as we walked along the street – we used to go into the shops to try and avoid them.

'One evening my husband and I went for a meal and a few drinks, and we were walking home at about 12.30 and guess what, we were joined by these dogs again. They all decided they wanted to fight and I was so scared I screamed and jumped into a ditch; my poor husband's face was a picture.

'Then from nowhere a big black Labrador turned up and he chased the other dogs away. We were stunned. My husband pulled me from the ditch and we started to walk back to our apartment. As we were walking, this black Labrador joined us and escorted us safely home. When we got back, I gave him a big fuss and a nice biscuit as a thank you. I was very grateful to this dog, and during the rest of the holiday he would sit by our balcony as if he were standing guard. As for the pack of dogs, we were not bothered by them again.'

Now we can just about believe that a cat or a dog might save a life. But our faithful friends come in all sorts of disguises as this next story illustrates. Chris wrote:

Rabbit Alert

'I've had house rabbits for years now, and I love them all dearly, but I am particularly attached to my male rabbit Starsky.

I am sure he thinks he's human, he's so chilled out and always ready for a cuddle.

'One day I was downstairs with my mum having a cup of tea and my two bunnies were upstairs in the bedroom with the TV on. Starsky came to the top of the stairs and kept banging his feet and staring down at me which was odd. Rabbits always thump their feet if there is danger so I decided to go and see if there was something the matter. Starsky came flying down the stairs, looked at me and started banging his feet again. I followed him up the stairs, wondering what on earth was so important, and came into the bedroom only to find my TV had blown up and was smoking very badly. The curtains were dangling over the back of the TV and I am sure that after another couple of minutes they would have gone up in flames.

'As soon as Starsky realized that I had the situation in hand, he instantly "chilled out" and lay down in the corner of the room with the other bunny, and watched as I sorted it all out.

'I am sure that we would have had a nasty fire, had it not been for Starsky demanding my attention! Sometimes I wonder if he is my angel ...' So rabbits can be heroes too!

Okay, I'll admit it. This next story isn't an animal guardian angel story or anything like it but it was such fun, I thought I would share it with you just the same. Like the 911 cat story, this little tale also got a lot of press at the time.

Chimney Fish

Stunned pensioner, ex-miner Bill Brooks told the press how a ten-inch goldfish dropped down his chimney, and right into his blazing fire. But strangely enough, the fish actually lived to tell the tale. Bill was amazed as the soot-covered fish bounced out of the fire and onto his hearth.

Bill put the fish into a bath of warm water and fed it some bread, and right away it started swimming around. Bill clearly has a sense of humour as he called the fish Wanda, because he says it's a wonder it survived.

Bill believes that the fish was probably dropped down the chimney by a passing heron, so was lucky to be alive!

Perhaps the 'fish called Wanda' had her own guardian angel after all.

Here's Jo's story. When Jo was feeling lonely and sad at school, Ollie the hamster saved the day … from the other side.

New Friends

'I had a really nice hamster called Ollie. He was an albino Syrian, with little brown splodges and pink ears. He was a real little escape artist when he was younger, even ending up in the fridge! He lived for about four years, and it really broke my heart when he died.

'I'd spend every evening talking to him and playing with

him. He tried to talk back by making little quacking sounds. He was my best friend, really. I was having a terrible time at school, and he was the one who helped me through it. I felt really guilty about his death, as the day before I'd run home crying after a really bad day at school and just went straight to bed. I didn't talk to him, or scratch his tummy.

'In the morning, he was dead. I had to go to school, so I went with bright red eyes, all depressed and everything. At break time I thought I saw Ollie, so I ran after him. After all, I had no friends, why should I care if I looked a complete "nutter" running after what looked like my dead hamster? I lost him in a group of people, who realized I was crying and looked after me. They became my friends, and I'm now happy at school.

'I think it was Ollie who led me to them, as an angel. He knew he was my only friend, and so decided to find me some people who would be my human friends. He clearly forgave me for not talking to him that night. I still love him so much, and miss him. But I'm sure he was an animal angel.'

Once again, it seems as if the angels helped by borrowing our animal friends. Ollie led Jo to find the new friends she clearly needed in her time of grief and sadness.

We've seen just a few special animal stories here, and of course there are many more the world over. Do you own an angel pet? Has a pet touched your life or saved your life? The special love that exists between pets and their owners is the same as that between humans. Love carries across all boundaries of life and the afterlife. Our animals really are our special angels on earth.

Let's look now at some special stories involving children.

CHAPTER 14

Children's Heavenly Gifts

Every child comes with the message that
God is not yet discouraged of man.

Rabindranath Tagore

Many people believe that children who are being born into the world today are angels sent from heaven to save us from ourselves, to protect the human race from total destruction in the future. 'Crystal Child' and 'Indigo Child' are names used to describe children with these special psychic abilities. Another name sometimes used is 'Rainbow Child', and the terms all refer to the aura colours, or colours of the energy field which surrounds these children.

Are all children being born with special skills and abilities? It's hard to tell but I do have a large postbag which includes stories of young children with extraordinary abilities. Many seem to bring with them a strongly enhanced 'sixth sense' or increased natural psychic ability. They seem to be able to see, hear and pick up on information which to the rest of us appears extraordinary. Is this part of the natural evolution of humankind, or is it something else?

Children and animals have more in common than you might think, and as in the previous chapter about animal angels, they seem to have a mutual understanding of each other.

This story really caught my eye.

Animal Magic

'How aware is a newborn baby? As a grandmother, I have experienced a psychic communication with my grandchild. My granddaughter is about three months old.

'One day, we took her to the zoo. It was a big surprise to witness the baby and the spotted otters communicating with each other. The animals and the infant seemed to be communicating in a mind-to-mind way and they both seemed fascinated with the other.

'The child's parents are both psychics and so are most of their family. Before she was born, the baby seemed to be communicating with her family and they seemed to be able to communicate with her. In a way, it seems my granddaughter is fortunate in that her family is open to the concept of psychic activity and other areas which many families seem to fear. Perhaps, this openness will help her develop her own natural skills as she grows and matures.

'The thought has crossed my mind recently as I have observed my own grandchild. What if all children had an open, supportive environment to develop their own natural psychic abilities? Would more children show signs of being psychically gifted? How important is a supportive environment to psychic development?

'Personally, I think it is very important for natural child development, let alone psychic awareness and development. People are naturally psychic and have these skills, yet many of them do not develop their natural skills due to peer pressure, family disbelief, or lack of support.'

I agree totally. Here is another great story about children and animals.

Tuning into the Kittens

'A couple of weeks back my cat gave birth to kittens in the basement of our house. That morning everyone got up as usual, drank coffee, made breakfast, etc. No one went to the basement to check on the cat to see if the kittens had been born.

'My mother and two-year-old son were sitting at the table when my son suddenly said, "Babies," and pointed towards the floor.

'My mother asked him, "What babies?" He again pointed to the floor and said, "Kitties." My mother asked him, "Did Grey Cat have her kitties?" He yet again pointed to the floor and said, "Cat." So my mother went down to the basement and there were two kittens!'

I think like most children he is showing his natural intuition and with a little encouragement (whilst treating the ability as normal as possible), he will develop his psychic abilities at a nice gentle rate. I always advise parents to keep a record of any psychic experiences their children have, and to date their entries for future reference.

Of course, it is very important to let a child develop naturally. I get a lot of questions about children's psychic ability, and in fact run a 'psychic children' forum online. This free service is available so that parents and grandparents of naturally gifted children can talk about their experiences. Having a child with abilities outside the 'normal' can be a little frightening for the parents, especially when they have no experience in how to deal with the phenomenon at all.

There isn't a rule book, of course, and sometimes the best support can come from others who have been through the same experience. Rachael told me:

Crystal Child

'I am the mother of a six-month-old "crystal" child. He was born on Christmas Eve, and the moment he was born I knew there was something different about him. (I am not being biased since I think he is extra special already! But everyone comments on how alert, aware and adult he seems.)

'He is a typical crystal in that he is very advanced and seems like an adult in a six-month-old body. He has a very gentle nature but is very smart! I come from a line of natural intuitives – and I am an adult "indigo" and communicate with angels myself.

'I am very clearly able to communicate with my son without speaking. I also think he is telekinetic. He can turn his toys on and off from across the room without even touching them.

'On several occasions, whilst I was pregnant with him, I would be folding clothes in his room and preparing for him, when tiny orbs of light showered down in his room. It was spectacular. I knew it was his soul letting me know he was watching me, and preparing to incarnate on earth.

'On the morning of Christmas Eve the lights came down on me again whilst I was in the shower and I knew he would be born soon. I can't wait to watch him grow and help him on his spiritual path. I know why he chose me to be his mother because I am able to help him on this path. I myself was also a psychic child, as was my mom, both grandmas and great grandma.

'It is very important that we recognize our children's abilities as great gifts from God and not fear them because of all the Hollywood bologna! Communicating with spirit has occurred since the beginning of time, it is no different now. I tell my in-laws, "Why is it so strange that I can communicate with angels, but it isn't strange that many people in biblical times did also!" We all can, if we just learn to listen! It is so important because this new generation of children is helping to bring our world to a much higher spiritual dimension.

'These children are so amazing and although they may be young on earth they are very ancient and wise souls. We should be so honoured and blessed to care for them. I have read several comments in magazines where parents feel their children's actions are strange, scary or weird. Please try to understand it and be positive. Teach them to ask God and the angels for protection but to not show any fear of their gifts. Archangel Michael is a great protector, especially for children, and will always serve and protect if asked.'

The great Archangel Michael is easy for children to relate to. Michael's primary role is protection. Children can visualize Michael because he is usually pictured wearing a suit of armour and carrying a flaming sword. It is an easy leap of faith to believe that this great and powerful being is able to look after them. Archangel Gabriel brings gentle communication energy and often appears to children as a female angel. Archangel Raphael is the great angelic healer and Archangel Sandalphon looks after unborn children. Your children can work with all these angels and more.

Emma is a teenager now. She knows she had certain abilities as a young child but she also had her own guardian angel. This angel appeared to her as a male. Children see male figures when protection is required and usually female figures when gentle and comforting qualities are needed.

Burglars in the House!

'I'm lucky enough to have parents who completely accept a lot of the things I say; in fact, my mum has the natural ability to draw spirits towards her. Of course, sometimes this isn't good because it can upset her and she hasn't learnt much in the way of control over her abilities.

'When I was six we were visiting my great grandma. No one had told me she was really ill so I didn't know why we were there, but I had brought a pair of angel dress-up wings with me. Mam assumed it was for me to dress up in but apparently, I went over to my great grandma's bedroom door and, as I wasn't allowed in, I hung the wings on the door. When my mum asked what I was doing, I told her that the wings were for great grandma to go to heaven, and later in the night we had a phone call to say that she had died. Later, I went with my mum to view the body, and at nursery I had made a clay angel and I put it into her coffin with her.

'Then another time, when I was about eight years old, I woke up in the middle of the night for a drink of water. I remember that my older cousin Katie was staying over at the time. I went to the top of the stairs, but there was a white figure standing at the bottom, a man. He smiled at me and I felt calm and stayed at the top of the stairs ... but then he vanished as another man ran past him. It turns out that we were being burgled and if I had gone downstairs I may have been hurt. The weirdest part is, a few moments after I woke up, my cousin joined me, then my mum, and the only person who stayed asleep was my dad!'

Lots of children see angels. Best-selling author Cassandra Eason told me, 'My son Jack was five or six when he told me that there was an angel outside his bedroom window. He described it with wings and then said, "Do you think it is a wind up (clockwork) angel?" He had just started school and was being teased about his psychic powers.'

Cassandra has gone on to write many books relating to psychic subjects, including her book *The Psychic Power of Children*, which includes an experience I had myself as a child. This experience is one of several she went through when her children were younger, and like me, these experiences turned into a career!

Ria shared her very personal experience with me, to show that there is always light at the end of the tunnel.

Angel on a Bus

'When I was fourteen, something very bad happened to me – I was raped and I had to go for treatment at the hospital. One day I was on my way to the hospital with my dad to have my next course of injections when something strange happened. It was a bright and sunny day but to me it felt very dark and lonely, but that's probably why I didn't notice a lady on the bus ... that is, until she got up and moved near us.

'She smiled at me, and I felt very protected by this lady, especially with her sitting so close. This lady told me that things would be okay in the end, and I would get justice one day.

I wondered how she knew about what had happened to me and although she said it indirectly, somehow I knew she was talking about the rape so I opened up to her.

'The lady also went on to tell me that she was publishing a book and that I was to go and buy it at the weekend. We all got off the bus at the same stop and my dad and I said goodbye to this charming lady. She even kissed me on my cheek before we walked away. Suddenly I had a strong impulse to turn around and when I did the lady had disappeared. This left me totally dumfounded but not as dumfounded as I was when I went to buy the book on the Saturday. The shop worker searched and searched for the author and title, and found that the author had died many years before.

'Unfortunately, my parents stopped me from going ahead with the court case and I took her book as another hidden message. I am in the process of telling my story and writing a book about my experience, but I know that my angels have always been with me, just like they had been on the bus that day.'

Have you ever considered the possibility of reincarnation? There are many books on the subject, especially those that deal with young children who have memories of past lives. I love it when scientists follow up these children's stories, and it turns out that when a child remembers a past-life family in a remote village, many miles from their home, things are exactly as the child 'remembers' from the past life. Some are even saying that they have now 'proved' that reincarnation exists by following up these case histories.

Other children seem to know information about members of their own 'soul groups', and tune in to their future lives.

I remember my daughter walking into the room and telling me very calmly, 'Great Granny can't come and visit us any more because she is going to be born again to another lady.' Well, my grandmother had been dead for several years and my daughter was just a few months old when she passed over. We always felt that she was around us but I don't remember that we ever mentioned this to my daughter. Later, I decided to question her about what she had said but she had no memory of the conversation at all. So perhaps Great Granny had left for her new body after all – who knows!

When I read the following story I immediately thought of my own experience.

Born Again

'I was spooked out the other day by my four-year-old son who started talking about my nan, who died in May 2004. Out of the blue he said that Nanny in Heaven was going to be born again and that she was a new baby growing in a lady's tummy now. He told me that when she is born we won't know her because she will be a baby, but it will be Nanny that has come back.

'I was thrown by this as reincarnation is not something we talk about in front of the children. I asked him who had told him that, and he said no one, he just knows. So I explained to him that some people believe that it does happen and that if it does, it is a lovely thing, and he was happy with that.'

Karen believes that her daughter's guardian angel sent her a premonition which prevented her daughter from getting hurt. She told me:

Angels Sent for Mum

'My eldest daughter Laura, aged fifteen, was going through a pretty rough time at school a few months back. She was getting bullied a lot and one particular day I sent her to the shop to get some milk. After about five minutes I got an urge to go and make sure she was okay. I had a real "gut feeling" that something was wrong, so I put on my shoes and coat and went to find her. It was a good job I did, because there were six girls around her, and they were just about to beat her up!

'Even when I tell the children off for one thing or another, a voice pops into my head and tells me if I went a bit "over the top", and it certainly tells me if it doesn't agree with something I have said or done. It seems like my children's angels are very vocal.'

Let's look at more children's psychic abilities. This next story is very sad but the children had been prepared by the other side.

I Might Need My Watch

'My second daughter (when she was a pre-schooler) told us which day of the week that my mother-in-law would pass away, so we know that she is a "sensitive". My youngest daughter came to me two days before my husband's (supposedly simple) surgery and said that her grandmother had visited her (her grandmother had passed away when she was just one year old). She described her as a younger woman, but my husband recognized the description right away.

'Her grandmother told her, "We are sorry, we don't know what went wrong with the surgery," and that, "we are waiting for John." Knowing her psychic abilities, this alarmed us, and we prepared as best we could. Both girls were very anxious about his surgery and didn't like the "darkness growing" in and around Daddy.

'John's simple benign tumour was diagnosed as Stage Four terminal cancer, which had spread to his lungs, liver and more. They (his daughters) knew he was dying before the doctors did. Six months, the doctors say. Less, according to our daughters, but we don't press them.

'Laughter is the best medicine, so I will leave you with this: Ally warned me that Dad would be angry about his vitals. (It made no sense at the time.) At the hospital, my husband was in a morphine fog when I told him, "Honey, I took your watch, your ring and your wallet. I have them." He responded, "Okay, but the nurse just took my vitals (meaning vital signs: blood pressure, pulse, etc) and I want them back, I might need them!"

'He will leave us laughing to the very end.'

I contacted this lady again recently and her husband's time of passing was very close. The children had been right. But the whole family know that their grandmother is waiting for him with open arms.

Sheryl's daughter also saw her grandmother.

Hi Grandma

'Yesterday, my daughter Kara was playing as any typical child would (she is not typical, but for those around her, she appeared to be at that moment). She is six, and she suddenly looked up with a startled expression on her face as she exclaimed excitedly, "Mama, mama, look, it's your mother, it's your mother ... look!"

'I could not see her, of course, and Kara could, which really freaked me out. She had a look on her face that said "Doesn't everyone see her?"

'Later, I asked many details about my mother and she described her beautifully.'

Young children seem to have amazing mediumistic abilities, pre-schoolers in particular. Sadly, unless they are supported at home, many children lose this ability once they start school and begin lessons. In schools we are taught a different way of learning about the world, and children soon discover how to keep quiet about skills which other children do not have. Teasing is a great way of shutting down psychic skills ... sadly.

Are some children's invisible friends actually make-believe? Perhaps not.

Make-Believe Friends?

'We realized our five year old had psychic abilities and that they had started around age two and a half. He has a group of "angels" that are always with him. Two boys and two girls. The two girls are his age and he says that they are actually my children but they live in heaven. Interestingly, I had two miscarriages before I had him, so perhaps he is right.

'The other two children are boys that have "found" us because we have a happy home and they like to play with my son. They all have names and my son says they like to play while he is sleeping. He is very matter of fact when he talks about them.'

In most cases, psychic ability in a child can be a great asset, but there are odd cases where a child's paranormal abilities can cause disruption in a home. Often these come as a result of children with disabilities which can often go hand in hand with psychic ability. These children can also be very clever, but not in a conventional way. For the parent, it can be a bit of a challenge. Sue from the Oregon told me:

Psychic Boy

'My son is now six years old and the "orbs" (balls of light) started appearing at around five years old, although we didn't notice them until recently. I have tons of photos taken of my son surrounded by these white circular lights.

'He always spoke of ghosts, but I put them down to his imagination. In November his descriptions of "ghosts" drastically changed. His TV started switching on in the middle of the night to the static channel, and even the cats wouldn't go into his room. We had to smudge* and salt the room and place crystals in there to help him feel empowered and safe.

'He continues to see them, and recently talked of "spirits". We found out last week that these "spirits" are his guides, but he originally perceived them as a threat. We now take him to a spiritual healer who tries to help him understand what is happening, and he loves going to see her.

'We've had to smudge a couple of times now, but don't do his room without him now because I believe he should be active in controlling his world. He can see auras around people, and will comment about people on the street, and about what "colour" they are, even though they aren't physically wearing this colour.

'He is extremely sensitive (and always has been) and internalizes all negative energies. He knows when people are upset, hurt or emotional, and begins to display the behaviour which he senses around himself. It can be very confusing for me because at times I don't understand where the emotion is coming from and it can take a long time to get the story out and understand why he's acting the way he is.

'He has up and down days like most kids, but he gets depressed really easily. I try to get him to talk about what he's feeling but sometimes he won't talk. He is ADHD (Attention Deficit Disorder) and is on medication, but not too much because I don't want it to drone him out. He has enough just to get through school and daycare.

'His medication was the only thing that got him through writing the alphabet for the first time! We had been working on him for a long time and he never got past the letter P. Day two on the right dose and he started writing the whole alphabet. I didn't even think he knew that much since we'd never covered it.

'He is extremely smart, outgoing and full of love. He gets along with almost everyone and doesn't understand why people fight. He is a very special boy. He has talked about flying in his dreams, so I can only assume that he is having out of body experiences. He has great fascination with rocks, crystals, water and dirt, although who doesn't?

'Sadly he hasn't made that many friends. He's had incidences where other kids have called him weird and names due to his abilities, and of course he believes them. I had to sit down and do some exercises with him to show him how wrong these other kids were, and that they just don't understand.

'I have told him that maybe, for now, he should keep his

special experiences to the family only, that is, until he develops a close relationship with someone he can trust.

'One thing that helped was to write a list of things that he is good at, and what makes him so unique. He keeps his list by his bed and we go over it together when he's feeling low.

'He's so good when someone is ill. He has a sort of natural instinct for it. When someone is sick, he goes to them and either sits practically on their lap, or places his hands on them. It's very interesting to watch. He first did this to me when I was ill with meningitis and focused on my head and spine, even though no one had told him to do this. He was only two then!'

* Smudging is a traditional cleansing ritual performed to clear spirit energy (particularly negative energy) from a room. The smudge is made up of bundles of dried sage, usually white sage, and sometimes mixed with other things like lavender or sweetgrass. The dried herb bundles are lit and then the resulting smoke is wafted around the room. Smudge sticks are available from most new age stores and over the internet.

Tracey told me that she has occasional problems with spirits around her children. It's as if these energies are desperate to communicate and realize that the children can see them. Not all children want to chat with the other side. Tracey told me, 'With both of my sons I have told them that if the spirits that are visiting them are not surrounded by the white light or by God's light, then they are to tell them to go away and not come back. I also pray with the kids about this and ask that their guides and mine will make sure this happens.'

Several people have told me that this works well. Just asking spirits to 'go away' strongly is usually all it takes. By far the most visiting spirits are either relatives, friends or guardian angels of the child anyway, so there is normally no reason to worry. Others are usually energies (ghosts) that are unaware that they are dead or are just attracted to the place where they died.

In almost all cases we are frightened because we don't know what we are dealing with. We can't 'see' these energies like we can other objects around us.

It's interesting how some children, as I did myself, experience their own special guides and angels as a threat initially, for this reason. Once they are aware that they are protected and loved by these energies, the fear usually goes away. Amy told me:

Seeing Spirits

'I think my young daughter Caitlin is psychic but she is not even three yet. I know my house has a young ghost who comes regularly to visit us. It is the ghost of a young girl who was four when she died two years ago in the bath. I know this because I have seen her. Caitlin has told me that she won't have a bath and when I asked her why, she told me the little girl said be careful or you will drown, but I have never mentioned the young girl to Caitlin and never told her what "drowning" is!

'She also tells me to carry her downstairs so that the man won't look at her. I have never seen this man but I know she wouldn't make it up. Now she tells me Lucy comes to play with her and her sister's toys, and we know this is true because sometimes we hear the toys going off on their own!'

Most children cope perfectly well with these experiences as long as we, the adults, handle them sensitively. As long as we don't show that we are frightened ourselves, and empower our children by telling them that they can ask the spirits to go if they want to, any initial problems usually disappear.

Being Nosy

Some children seem to have the ability to 'tune in' to their parents thoughts. This can be funny, but also annoying if we are having private thoughts! I remember one of my own daughters doing this – asking me a question about something that I hadn't mentioned out loud. This story is very similar.

Listening In

'I am the mother of two children. I feel that they are both somewhat psychic. Starting a few weeks ago, my son regularly looks up at the ceiling and says that he sees an angel. He said that his departed great grandmother is an "angel", so perhaps this is who he sees.

'When I ask what the angel said, he often just mumbles as if he doesn't really understand. We've discovered that our son has had some speech delays, although he talks okay now. I think we didn't realize earlier that he had speech delays because we were able to understand everything that he wanted without him saying a word. We were able to pick up on his thoughts.

'When he was a baby, he would wake up crying if either my husband or I had a bad dream.

'My daughter has been reading my mind a lot lately. She sometimes asks me questions about a topic I am thinking about without me ever mentioning it. I was thinking about someone, and she repeated the name several times without hearing it from me or knowing who it is. Then, on another occasion, I was reading a chapter about Joseph, and she decided to watch the story of Joseph on video. It was a video that she'd owned for a long time and hadn't watched for ages, so it was a strange coincidence.'

Lindy from South Africa has a very positive outlook to her child's experiences and handles them well.

Visit from God

'My four-year-old son Garrett refuses to sleep over at my brother and sister-in-law's house as he battles to sleep because there are too many people that "talk" to him.

'After one particular sleep-over session (before he told me about "the people") he came home stuttering so badly that he could not put two words together, yet prior to that he didn't have a speech problem at all. About a week or so later he came to me and said that he would like to talk to me. After a very slow start he told me that God had come to visit him at his aunt's house, but would not elaborate.

'After yet another sleep over, he told my husband that there are too many people that talk to him at night and that they keep him awake.

'It was around the same time that I was inexplicably drawn into a book shop to find something of interest to read, and without hesitation I walked to the spiritual section and picked up your book *An Angel Treasury*. Having given this all some thought I have decided that "someone" is trying to show me something that I need to know. Now I have read up on the subject more I am able to help my son with his abilities. From someone who did not know much about the spiritual world, this has been an enlightening path that has brought me great peace and happiness.'

As parents, we can learn as much as possible about our own children's gifts and how others cope. It's a big learning curve because each child is individual. Our own actions and reactions make the difference between a calm and together psychic adult or one who is burdened; or one who has to keep their experiences a 'secret' because those around them do not believe what they see and hear, or worse, call them liars.

As parents, we can better help our psychic children by learning about the different types of psychic ability and what they mean:

- 'Clairaudience' is the ability to hear outside of normal parameters (clear hearing)
- 'Clairvoyance' is psychic vision (clear sight)
- 'Clairsentience' is the ability to pick up things using psychic sense (clear sensing)
- 'Clairgustance' or 'Clairalience' is psychically picking up smells
- 'Clairambience' is psychic taste.

Other areas for investigation might include out of body experiences (lots of children have these) and telepathy (mind-to-mind communication).

Kay's daughter 'remembers' an experience from the past. The only thing was, she wasn't born at the time!

Vision from the Womb?

'My little girl had a strange dream the other day. She dreamed of a car wreck which involved me, my three older boys, and my two friends. Her dream was correct right down to the last moment of her dream, where she saw me in the emergency room lying on a stretcher, whilst the doctors were sewing me up with glass still in my side.

'Strangely, I was three months pregnant at the time this happened, and my daughter was still inside me at the time the car accident occurred. I believe my daughter has a gift; also, orbs always appear with her in photographs, or we see them around her. To have a child like this is a BLESSING ... enjoy them.'

A blessing indeed. Do your children show psychic abilities? They are not alone, and my research does seem to indicate that more and more children are born with enhanced intuition of various kinds. Perhaps, after all, this is just the natural development of the human soul.

CHAPTER 15

Somebody Helped Me

Be not forgetful to entertain strangers, for thereby some have entertained angels unawares.

Hebrews 13:2

'Angels' come in many disguises. There is the stranger who stops along the roadside and helps with your broken-down car before disappearing into the night; and there is Great Grandma, who yells at you to put your brakes on, seconds before you are going to be hit by that large truck. Maybe your angel comes to you dressed in white and appearing in regular dreams? Is your angel your child or your pet?

We've looked at a wide variety of stories in this book and studied in depth the afterlife communication phenomenon. I hope you feel comforted that life goes on and we are never alone. Angels, guides and our departed loved ones are always around when we need them, and when they can't be with us, they send a 'stranger': a neighbour, a friend, a child or even a pet.

There are a few more stories that I would like to share with you. They are all experiences which stood out in my mind and I felt really strongly that I should include them here. Some are sad and some are happy. One is even quite shocking, but it is important that you see things how they really are.

My 'Guardian' Watching Over Me

'As a special needs tutor it is my job to teach children and teenagers who are too ill to attend school, or have been excluded for bad behaviour. One of these was Ricky, a fifteen-year-old who was a member of a paramilitary organization.

'One morning he told me about his troubles (several boys had threatened to beat him up and he was terrified), and eventually he settled down to some written work. As he worked I saw a golden angel bend over him and enfold him. Then the angel looked at me and said, "I'm Stanley."

'I was amused at the name and told Ricky what I had seen.

'He was cheered by this and later as I was leaving he excitedly started to tell his mother what had happened. When he got to the point about the angel's name, his mother's eyes filled with tears. She explained that Stanley had been her father's name and he had died before Ricky was born.'

These simple stories do change lives, and remain in the memory forever.

Jade's Angel Playing Chess

'When I was around seven years old I went to bed just as normal. Nothing was different at all about this day, and I fell asleep as I always did. Then, during the night I awoke from my sleep and at the end of my room sat an angel with a golden glow. I wasn't scared at all. The angel was female with very long, pleated hair, and had large wings.

'What was strange about this, though, was that she was sat playing chess and did not seem to be aware that I was awake staring at her. As suddenly as I awoke, I drifted back to sleep again. I can't make sense of this at all and when I tell people about my experience, they say I must have been dreaming but I know I was awake. I am now twenty years old and I still think about this experience a lot.

'My sister also claims to this day that she saw a cherub-like vision when walking up the hall in that same house. So the fact we both had experiences that were similar in such a short space of time confirms that this experience was very real for me and I feel really lucky that this happened, although I still have no idea why.'

Nikki's angel saved her in the most dramatic way.

Somebody Saved Me

'I have to tell you about my own experience regarding angel intervention.

'I had lots of paranormal experiences as a child and went through a period of two years between the ages of four and six of regularly seeing spirits and actually communicating with one, although I wasn't allowed to talk about it at the time. As a result of that, I dismissed my visions and other experiences, thinking that I was maybe hallucinating!

'When I was eighteen, my friend Sarah and I were travelling to Holdenby House in England (where the film *Biggles* was made). Sarah's auntie was the housekeeper at the time, and was holding a spiritual evening there in one of the great halls.

'It was dark and we were late and Sarah was pushing her Citroën CV to its limit around the narrow country lanes. All of a sudden we shot over a major road (we had not noticed the junction). Time slowed down as we floated in slow motion above the road, looking down at the headlights of the cars whizzing underneath us! We then landed with a bounce onto the narrow road which continued after the junction. We both looked at each other stunned and said, "What was that?" just like you mentioned in your book! We knew that an angel must have ensured our safe landing!'

Often, even when these magical things are happening to us, it seems very bizarre, if not surreal. We know something has happened but it seems so strange that our brains have difficulty with accepting what we know to be true. Luckily, in this case, Nikki was not alone and shared the experience with someone else.

Jill saw her sister several times after she passed over. The experience helped her to heal and move on.

God Let Me Come and Visit

'My sister Jane was twenty-four when she was told she had cancer. There was nothing the doctors could do for her and she died ten months later. Her death affected all the family and it was such a shock for us all. The day of the funeral came … I had never been to a funeral before and I certainly didn't expect it to be my sister's. I remember it being a really hot summer's day. The sky was clear blue and the sun shone down. I thought that this was because my sister was in heaven and it gave me some comfort.

'After the funeral I went home, and later went to bed; after the long day I fell asleep quickly and had my first dream. All I could see was a field with a tree and then I could see Jane. It was just her face, and she was smiling. She was so happy, something we hadn't seen for a long time (she hardly ever smiled during her illness).

'When I woke the next day I felt some comfort, but remember thinking that she was telling me that she is at peace, no longer in pain. After I had taken my children to school I received a phone call from my mum. She was crying, and I assumed she was still upset from the previous day, until she told me that my nan (her mum) had died too. She had suffered a heart attack the afternoon we buried my sister. Mum had only just found out because no one knew how to tell her;

she had just lost her daughter, and now her own mum had died, it was so awful.

'Nan had been out watering her flowers when the attack had happened. After speaking to my mum, I realized that my dream of my sister smiling and happy was because she wasn't on her own. My nan was now with her, they were together and it brought me some comfort.

'Not long after that, I dreamt I was walking through a tunnel of mist or clouds. I then appeared in a hospital. I saw my sister, she was sitting in a chair, with her head resting on a table, covering her head with her hands, and she was crying. I asked her what was wrong and she said she didn't want me to see her without any hair. She had been having chemo (she never had chemo when she was alive because she was too weak). I sat with her and comforted her and then I left. It was like she was being treated on the other side and this was her way of showing me what was happening in a way that I would understand.

'The next morning I clearly remembered everything and felt that I had actually been there. I had another two dreams after this, and each time I went through this mist and arrived in this hospital. The second time my sister's hair was starting to grow back. She told me she was getting better, learning to walk again. She looked better, she was putting on weight and she looked really happy.

'The third time I went to the hospital, her hair had all grown back and it was long and golden like it was before. She was sitting on the edge of a hospital bed and above her bed was a picture. She said her children had drawn it and sent it to her (she had five children). On the bed was a new baby, a little girl, and she said it was hers. She was very happy, her cancer was gone and she could walk again (something she couldn't do when she got really ill). It was just wonderful!

'We sat talking. I told her about what had been happening while she was away and she told me not to worry because she could see everything that goes on in our lives.

'When I woke up I was just stunned. I feel and I am sure I really did go there, I don't know how or why but it was so real. It gives me comfort knowing that she is well and happy and can see all of us.

'One day, she surprised me and appeared in a dream in which I was just coming back from shopping with her little boy. When I got out of the car she was there, wearing her favourite clothes, smiling, looking beautiful. I asked her why and how she was here, and she said, "God has let me come down, to visit you for a little while," and that was it.

'In all of these "dreams" I have felt like they actually happened. I can remember them clearly. I often speak to my sister when I am down. I tell her to give my love to loved ones who are with her. I feel sometimes she is watching over me and my family, and I know one day we will be together again, because I believe that there is another life to which we will go next.

'Two or three days before my sister passed away something happened. It was evening and she was lying on her special bed that was in the living room, and her partner sat on the sofa in the same room. Then my sister sort of sat up and said she could see a girl sitting next to him. She kept asking him, "Who's that girl next to you?" and of course, he couldn't see anything. We always wondered if she had seen her guardian angel that evening.'

God seems to be letting lots of people 'see' their loved ones after they pass. The stories that people send me seem to be getting more and more complicated and elaborate. Are our worlds getting a little closer together, or is it that we are now more open to receiving an experience of this sort? Perhaps it's a little of both.

Rebecca's story is very powerful … and a little shocking, but I wanted to show you how strong the afterlife communication experience can be.

Seeking Justice from the Other Side

'I recently lost my cousin at the age of thirty-three, under very suspicious circumstances. He and I were very close. The interesting thing is, I have been having "afterlife dreams" for many years, but prior to his death and subsequently since then, I have received communication from him. He brings me very detailed information, and yesterday was no particular exception as we chatted for quite a while.

'I dreamt he and I were in a coffee shop when we began talking about his untimely recent death, and the mysterious circumstances in which it happened. He was very serious with me in describing how he died (suffocation), although the coroner has yet to rule on that. He said to me that his lover was responsible for his death, and described to me how desperately he had tried to leave his abusive partner, but to no avail.

'The week before he died I had visions of something terrible about to happen to him, and that he was in fear for his life. But at the time I did not know what that meant. Less than a week later I was notified by another family member about his sudden death.

'Anyway, my cousin was very descriptive and urgent with me about contacting his mother, and asking her to continue investigating his death and seeking justice for his murder. He also wanted to know whether his mother and stepdad still love him, and I reassured him that they still do, and are fighting for him to find resolution to this tragedy. He was very relieved to know that his mother still loves him, as they were not on speaking terms when he passed.

'He also conveyed messages for his stepdad and younger brother, which I gave them today when I spoke with my aunt. Towards the end of the conversation his sense of humour came out really strongly and we both had a hearty laugh. I hugged him, and assured him I would contact his mother right away. I asked him to promise me that he would talk to her soon and he said he would.'

Rebecca reassured me that although the contents of her visitation sound frightening, it was nothing like that at all. This story, like the one before, appears as if the loved one is visiting and chatting so completely normally it just seems beyond belief, but you and I already know that these experiences are all completely real.

Angels seem to be all around this family.

Family Angels

'Twenty-nine years ago something unexplainable happened to my daughter. I had just finished my ironing and had put the iron on the kitchen worktop. Quite foolishly, I had left the plug and flex hanging over the edge. I was in the garden hanging out more washing when I looked into the kitchen and saw my daughter, who was then about eighteen months old, pulling on the iron cord. I immediately ran towards the kitchen, knowing I would not get there in time to save her from the iron falling on her head.

'Suddenly the iron cord swung out of my daughter's hand and the iron went over her head, landing the other side of the kitchen. There is no way that the iron could have swung away from her like that and the family firmly believes that she was protected by an angel.

'Then years later, another incident happened. I was three weeks away from giving birth and in bed with my husband. I was feeling very low as my mother had died the week before from cancer after a long illness. My husband and I had argued over something silly and I was crying. My husband had a habit of smoking in bed, and he had one of those tall ashtrays on three legs. All of a sudden the ashtray, which was next to the bed, lifted approximately twelve inches from the floor and tipped all over onto my husband's pillow! It was surreal.

'There was no explanation for this at all. If the ashtray had tipped over it should have landed at the edge of the mattress and not on the pillow case. We tried several ways of knocking the ashtray over but could not come up with an explanation. A colleague of my aunt's was a medium and she said it was a warning not to smoke in bed.

'A couple of years later we moved house. One night, I woke up suddenly and turned on the lamp. The room was filled with smoke (there were no smoke detectors in those days). My husband had fallen asleep with a cigarette still alight and it had set the mattress on fire. Luckily, we were able to get our children out of their bedroom and my husband managed to put out the fire before it spread. We often wondered if this was our guardian angel too.'

So I guess the moral of the story is, always pay attention to your guardian angel's warnings!

Here is Vicky's story:

Saved from Drowning

'I am a psychic medium and have worked as a medium now for many years. It was a Sunday afternoon and my day off. I had worked all week and was very tired. Just as I finished cooking lunch, the telephone rang and it was a lady who seemed very desperate to see me. I explained very politely that this was my day off, and it was my time with the children. I even told her that she could phone me the next day and I would make an appointment with her then.

'This lady was very persistent ... rude even, and insisted that she needed to see me today. I explained again that it was my day off but after spending almost five minutes on the phone, she would not take no for an answer. It was really awkward but I finally managed to put the phone down.

'Afterwards, I couldn't stop thinking about this lady, so I pressed call back on my telephone to see where this call had come from. I noticed the code was almost an hour away.

'Just five minutes later, I had a knock on my side door. I looked through the kitchen window and could see a lady standing at my door and she was dressed all in black. I thought maybe she was lost, so I opened the door and actually asked her, "Are you lost?"

'It was the same woman who had been talking to me on the phone and she insisted that she see me. Well I was in shock! She was very tall and slim and I can remember her eyes because they were so blue.

'She told me she had a message for me and I was surprised. I am usually the one giving the messages. She told me that the message was from my father so of course I explained right away that my dad had died.

'But the woman said she knew this and added that he was with his dog Charlie. I had no idea who this stranger was but she asked me rather insistently to let her in, because she said, "I have come to save Jack." I didn't know what she could be talking about so I must have had a confused expression on my face! The only "Jack" I knew was my young nephew.

'She told me, "Yes, your sister is called Mandy and her husband is called Andrew. Call your sister now, Jack is in the pond!"

'I had no idea how I was going to pass on this weird message to my sister but the woman insisted that I telephone straight away. Even as I did so, the lady began to describe my sister's room. My sister picked up the phone and my heart was really pounding as I asked her, "Where is Jack?" My sister doesn't even have a pond but it turned out he was next door playing and they had a pond. My sister just ran off in a panic, dropping the phone and all the while, this woman was standing next to me. I could hear some shouting going off in the background, but I couldn't make out what it was. I could hear my sister's voice but as I looked up, the woman had disappeared. I ran to the door with the phone in my hand but there was no sign of this woman; no car, nothing. I wondered if I was going crazy!

'But then my sister came back to the phone and she was crying and crying, saying, "Thank God, thank God, Jack is okay." He had fallen into the next door neighbour's pond, and was saved by an angel ... a blonde lady with bright blue eyes that came from nowhere. It took us all some time to get over the shock of it, but all I have to say that when people say that angels can come in any disguise I know that this is true.'

'Members' of the earth are developing at a very fast rate. Our children are being born with pronounced psychic gifts and even rabbits are saving our lives! Magic and miracles happen every day … look for it.

Have you noticed the magic in your own life? I promise you it is there. Every day, a flower blooms, a butterfly opens its wings or a rainbow fills the sky. These are life's miracles. Live with your eyes wide open and enjoy every single moment, knowing that your angels, guides and loved ones on the other side are with you, holding your hand as you walk through each and every day of the wonder called LIFE.

May your angels always be '… at your side'.

P.S.

Although I had finished the book here, I felt that I should certainly add this little postscript. My lovely editor Fiona wrote me this email after her first edit of the book. Of course, the angels like to take their opportunities to make themselves known, when and where they can …

> 'Just a quick, hopefully amusing postscript – I had been working on your book for a few days, and went to Brighton to see my boyfriend last Tuesday. We were going to Stonehenge to watch the sunrise but, as it's World Cup time, we decided to watch the England–Sweden game in a nearby pub first. The pub was absolutely packed, and there was nowhere to sit.

Unfortunately, I have a problem with my sciatic nerve, which means that if I stand for too long, I am left in agony later. I was worried that standing for the whole game would mean that I would have a really hard time at Stonehenge, and decided to "test out" the angels! I quietly asked them to help me out, and lo and behold, the group of lads sitting right in front of the screen, about four feet away from us, just got up and left. How unlikely is that?

'Simon and I ended up with front row, comfy seats for the entire game, and when a couple of friends joined us, they had seats too! So thanks for reminding me about the angels; they allowed me to watch the footie and have a wonderful night and morning watching the sun rise at my favourite spot!'

Maybe I should have said, 'Remember to invite your passed-over loved ones *and* your angels into your life!'

About the Author

Jacky Newcomb is one of the UK's leading paranormal writers and angel experts. She has a great interest in angels, spirit guides, psychic children, afterlife communication and all things mystical and paranormal. She has had many paranormal and angel experiences during her own lifetime, many of which she shares here. She has studied a wide range of paranormal and psychic phenomena and holds a diploma in psychic development. Jacky is also a Reiki Master.

Jacky is the author of the hugely popular *An Angel Saved My Life*, her first collection of stories of the afterlife, as well as *An Angel Treasury* and *A Little Angel Love*. Her work has featured in the UK's foremost paranormal and mystical magazines including *It's Fate*, *Fate & Fortune*, *Prediction* and *Vision*. In addition she has produced features and articles for many non-paranormal women's magazines in the UK and around the world including *CHAT*, *My Weekly* and *Woman's Own*.

She runs several mystical 'agony aunt' columns and receives hundreds of queries and questions about paranormal experiences on her website and in response to her magazine and newspaper columns.

Jacky has acted as a consultant on several paranormal

shows and magazine features, and been interviewed on television programmes such as ITV's *This Morning* and LIVINGtv's *Psychic Live*. She is regularly interviewed on radio about her work.

Jacky is one of the presenters on the DVD *Angels* (for New World Music), and has recorded several guided meditations for Paradise Music. Signed copies of Jacky's books and other products are available at:

www.gabrielmedia.co.uk

Jacky runs an online angel and spiritual gift shop with her husband John and they live in England in a small Staffordshire village with their two daughters, their dog and a ginger tom cat.

For more information about Jacky and her work, visit her website, or write to her via HarperCollins (77–85 Fulham Palace Road, Hammersmith, London W6 8JB), remembering to enclose a stamped addressed envelope if you want a personal reply. Or, to ensure a reply, try e-mail, which is much quicker (jackytheangellady@yahoo.com)!

If you have uplifting and positive paranormal stories in your own life, then I would love to hear from you.

To contact Jacky online got to:

www.jackynewcomb.co.uk